46 Presidents

1. George Washington
2. John Adams
3. Thomas Jefferson
4. James Madison
5. James Monroe
6. John Quincy Adams
7. Andrew Jackson
8. Martin Van Buren
9. William Henry Harrison
10. John Tyler
11. James K. Polk
12. Zachary Taylor
13. Millard Fillmore
14. Franklin Pierce
15. James Buchanan
16. Abraham Lincoln
17. Andrew Johnson
18. Ulysses S. Grant
19. Rutherford B. Hayes
20. James A. Garfield
21. Chester A. Arthur
22. Grover Cleveland
23. Benjamin Harrison
24. Grover Cleveland
25. William McKinley
26. Theodore Roosevelt
27. William Howard Taft
28. Woodrow Wilson
29. Warren G. Harding
30. Calvin Coolidge
31. Herbert Hoover
32. Franklin D. Roosevelt
33. Harry S. Truman
34. Dwright D. Einsenhower
35. John F. Kennedy
36. Lyndon B. Johnson
37. Richard Nixon
38. Gerald Ford
39. Jimmy Carter
40. Ronald Reagan
41. George H.W. Bush
42. Bill Clinton
43. George W. Bush
44. Barack Obama
45. Donald Trump
46. Joe Biden

President Puppets

Instructions:

1. After photocoping, color in the head and the body of the president using colored penicls, crayons, markers, etc.

2. Cut out the parts carefully on the solid outline.

3. Glue the body of the president on the bag first.

4. Glue the head of the president onto the bottom flap of a paper lunch bag.

5. An optional **Quick Fact** writing sheet is also included which can be placed on the back of the president puppet.

You may adjust your photocoping to fit the different sizes of the lunch bag.

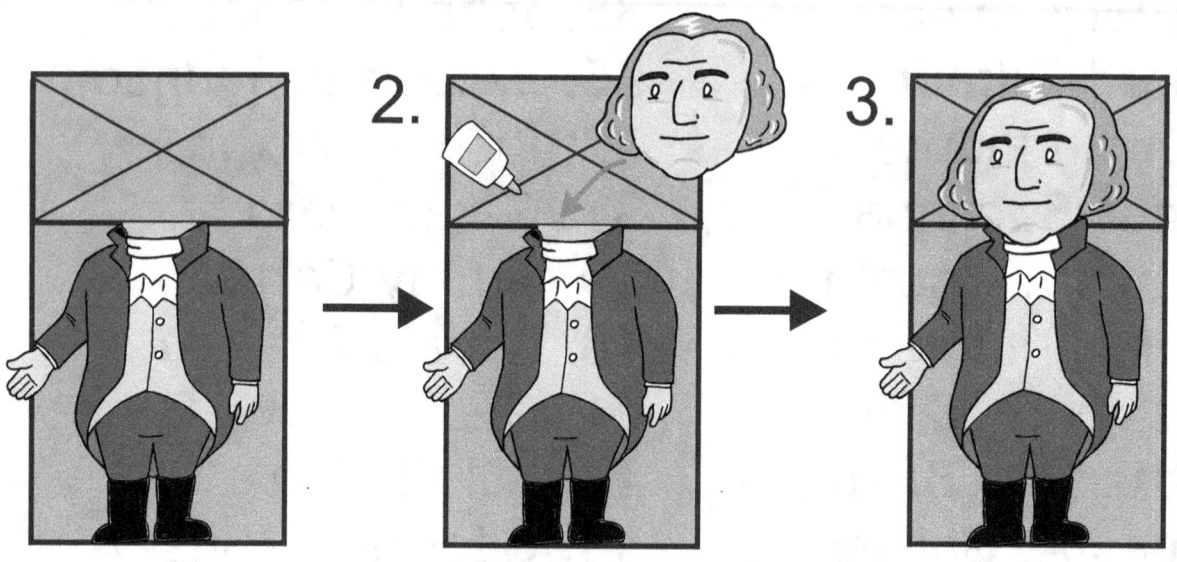

Copyright © 2022
All rights reserved. No part of this book may be reproduced by any means whatsoever without the written permission of the author.

Examples:

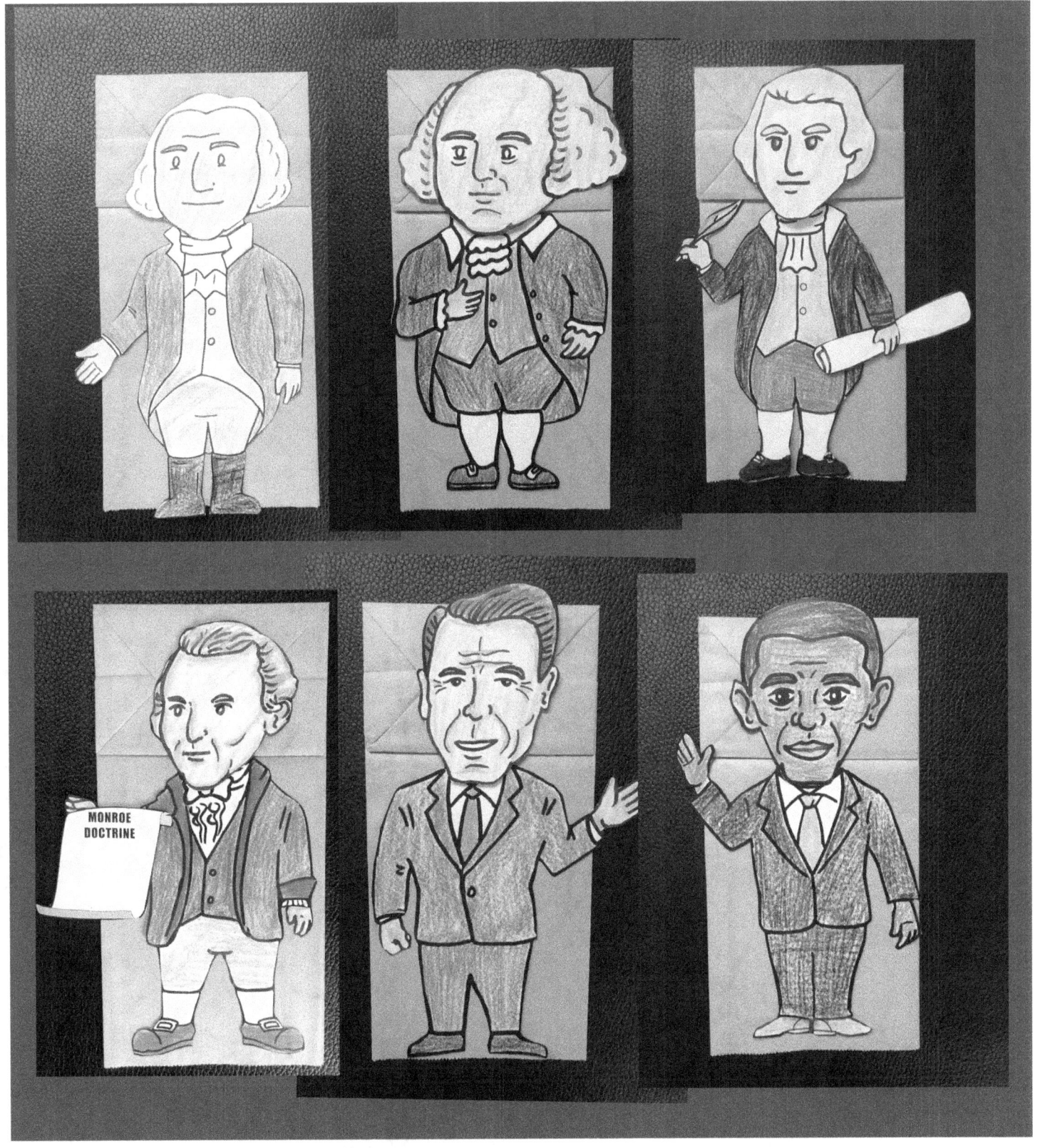

1. George Washington

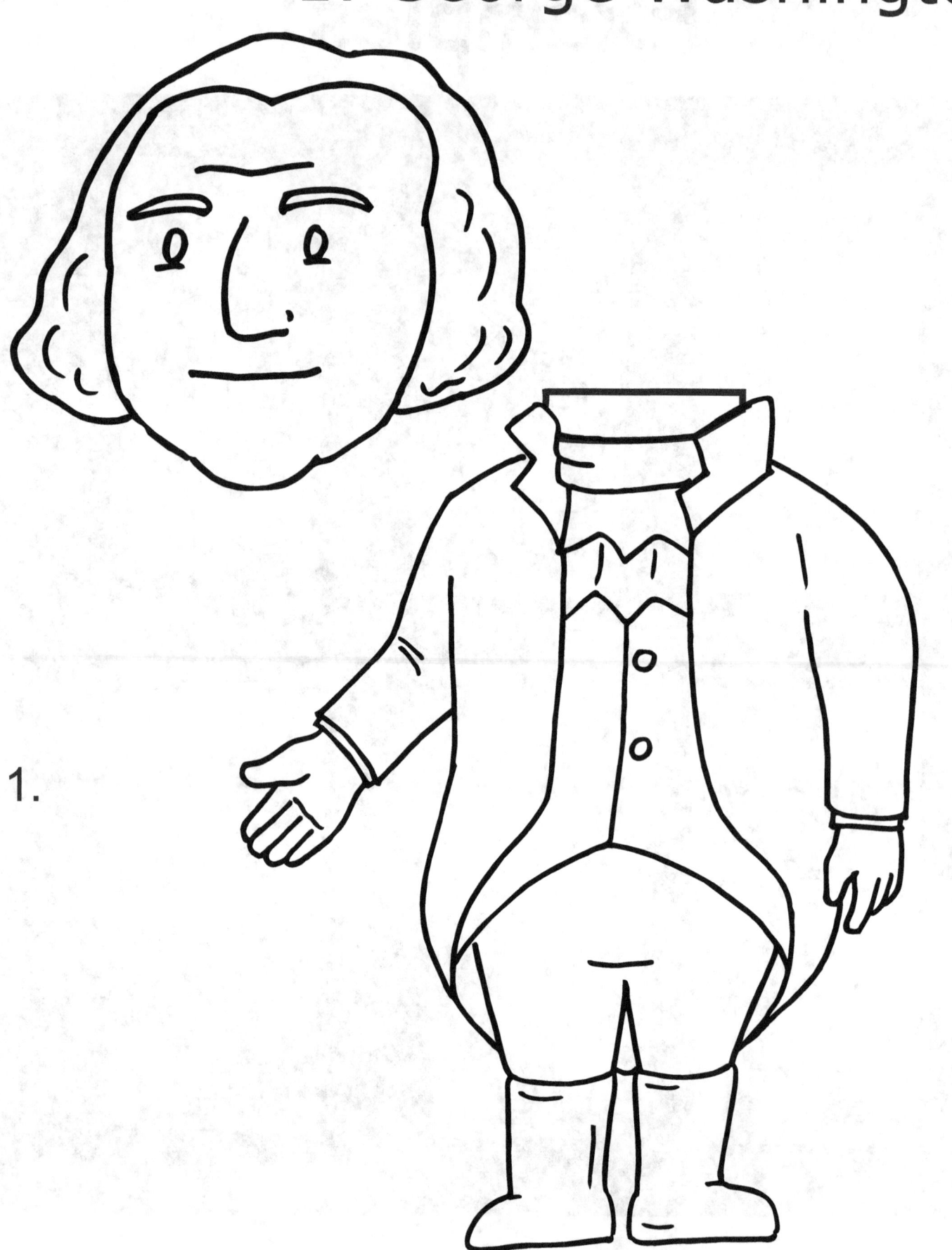

1.

2. John Adams

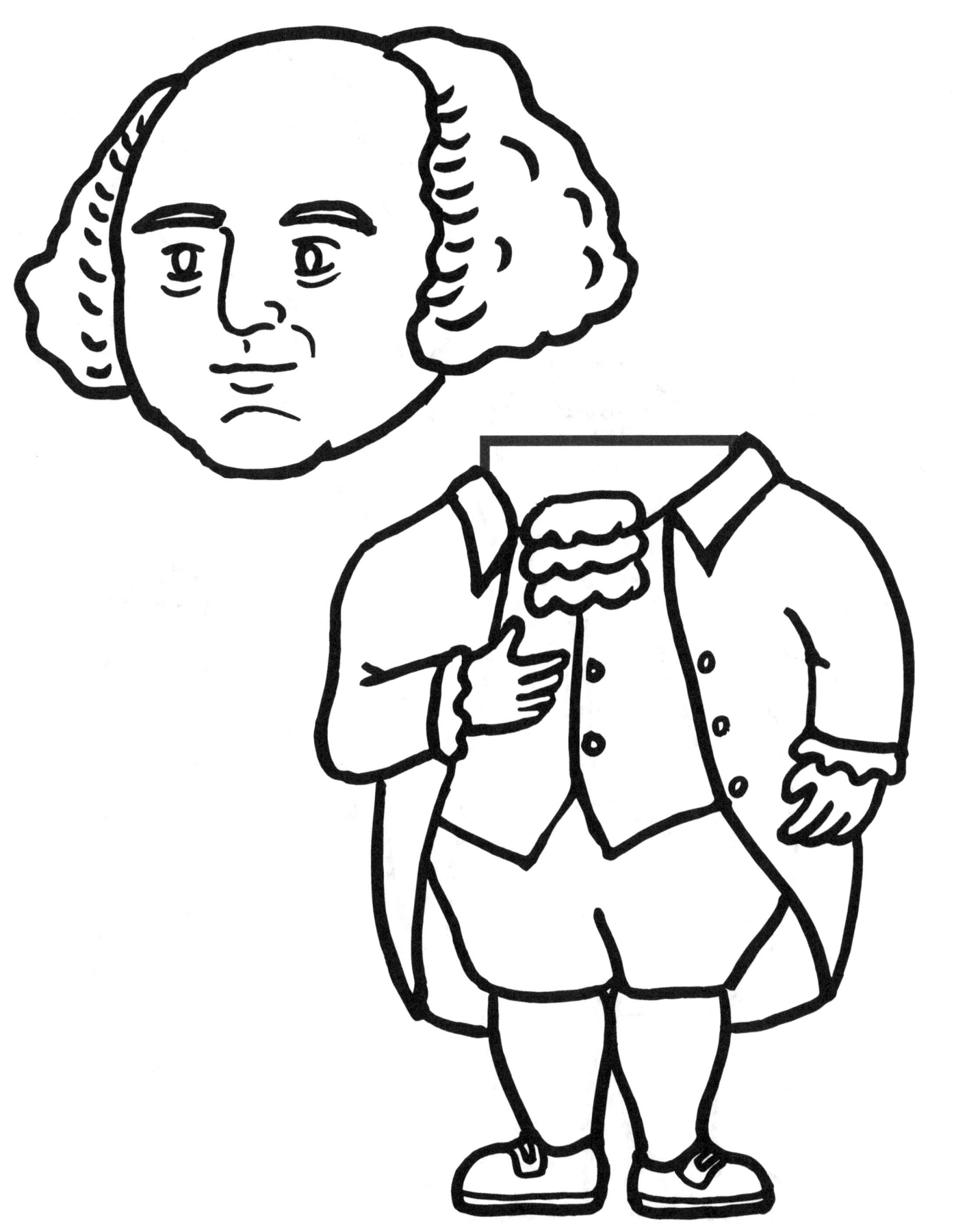

3. Thomas Jefferson

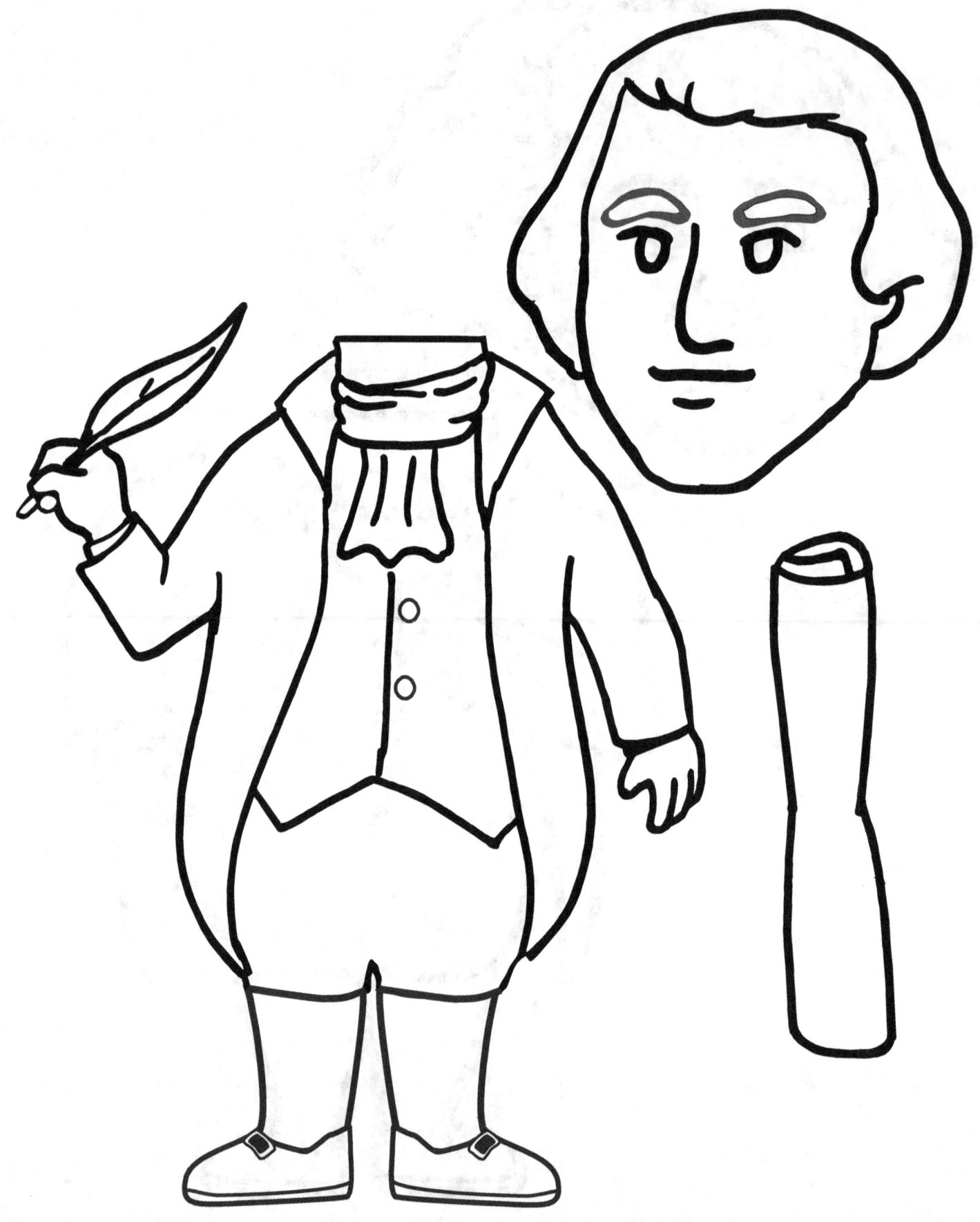

4. James Madison

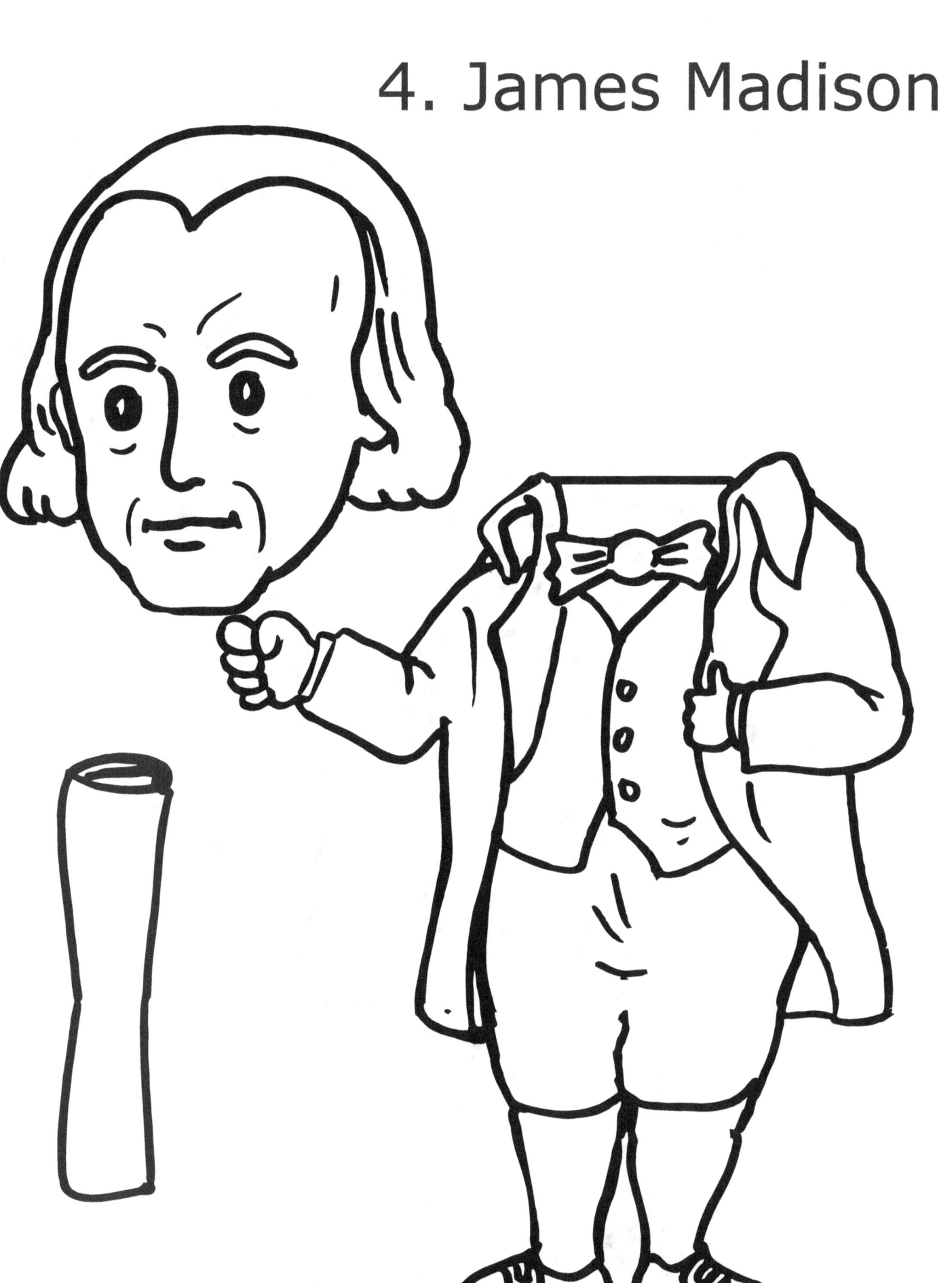

5. James Monroe

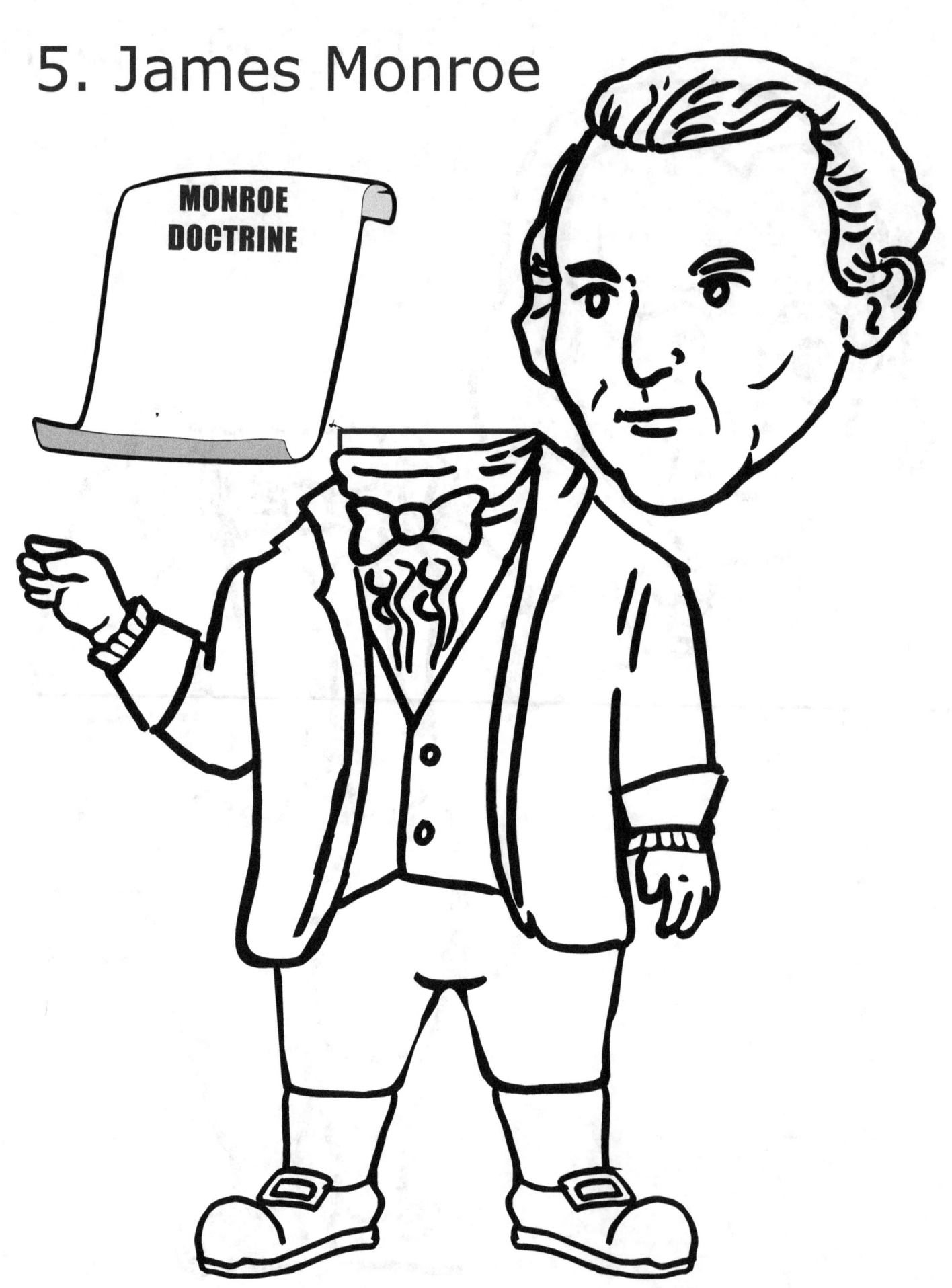

6. John Quincy Adams

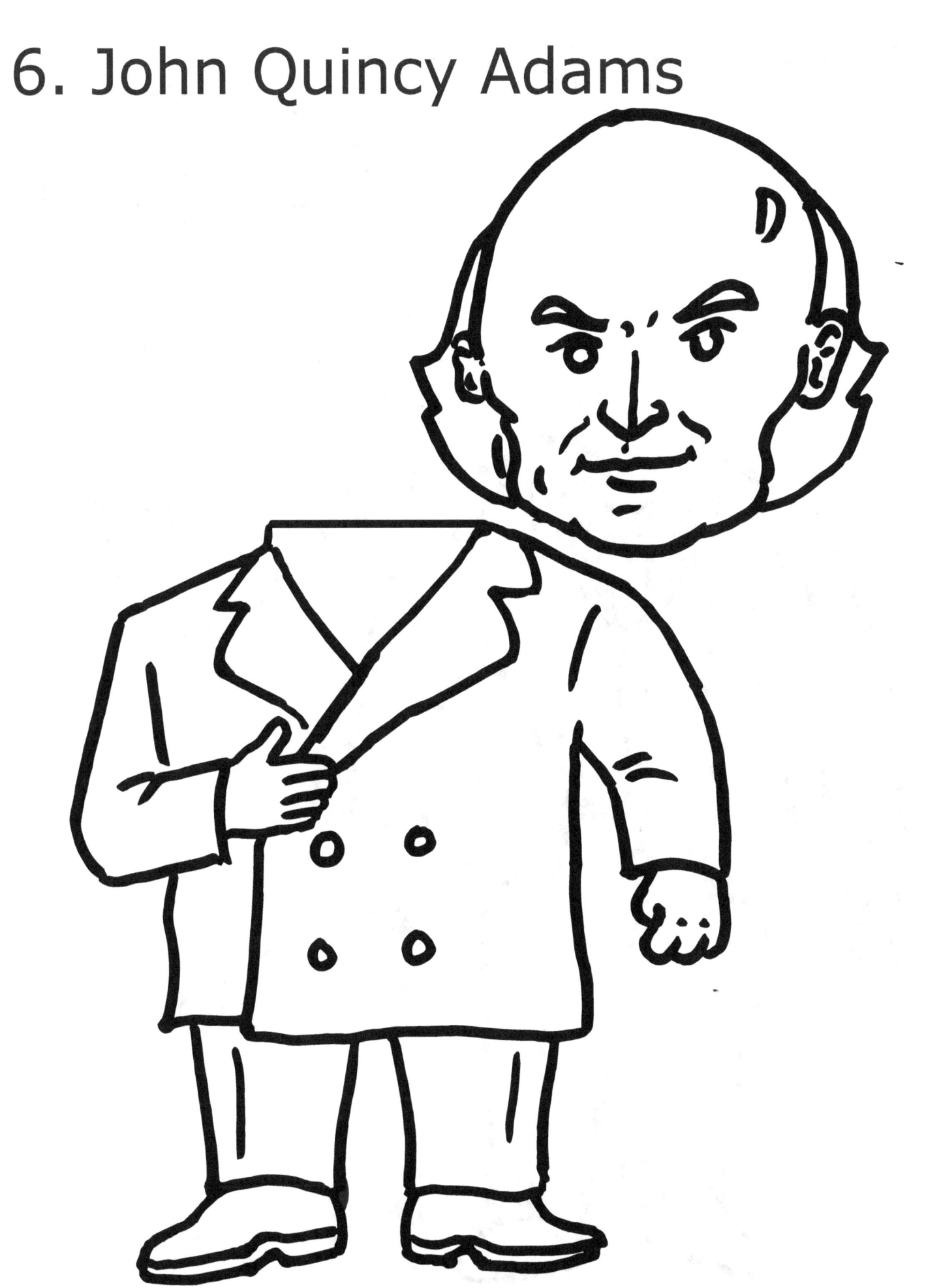

7. Andrew Jackson

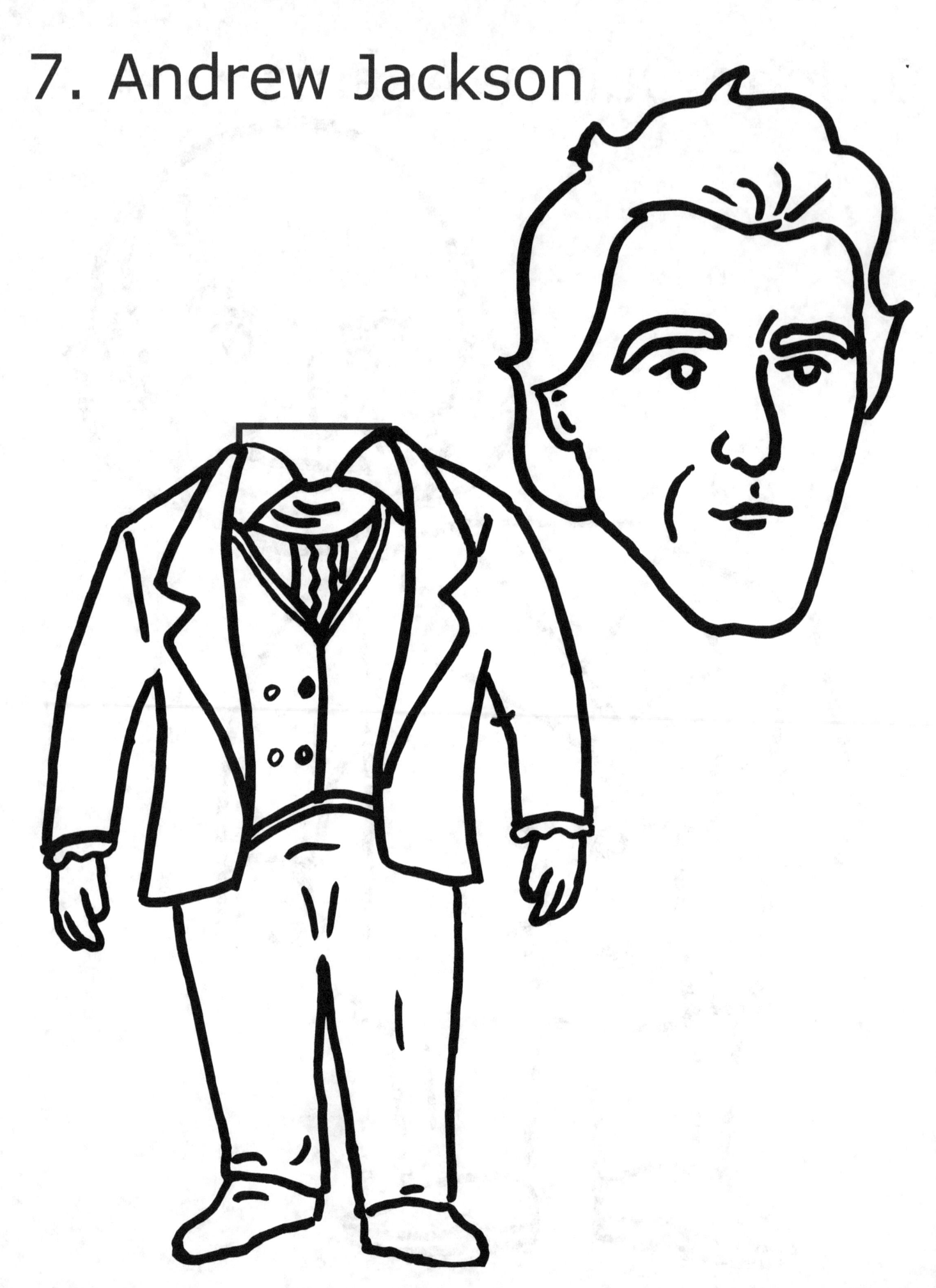

8. Martin Van Buren

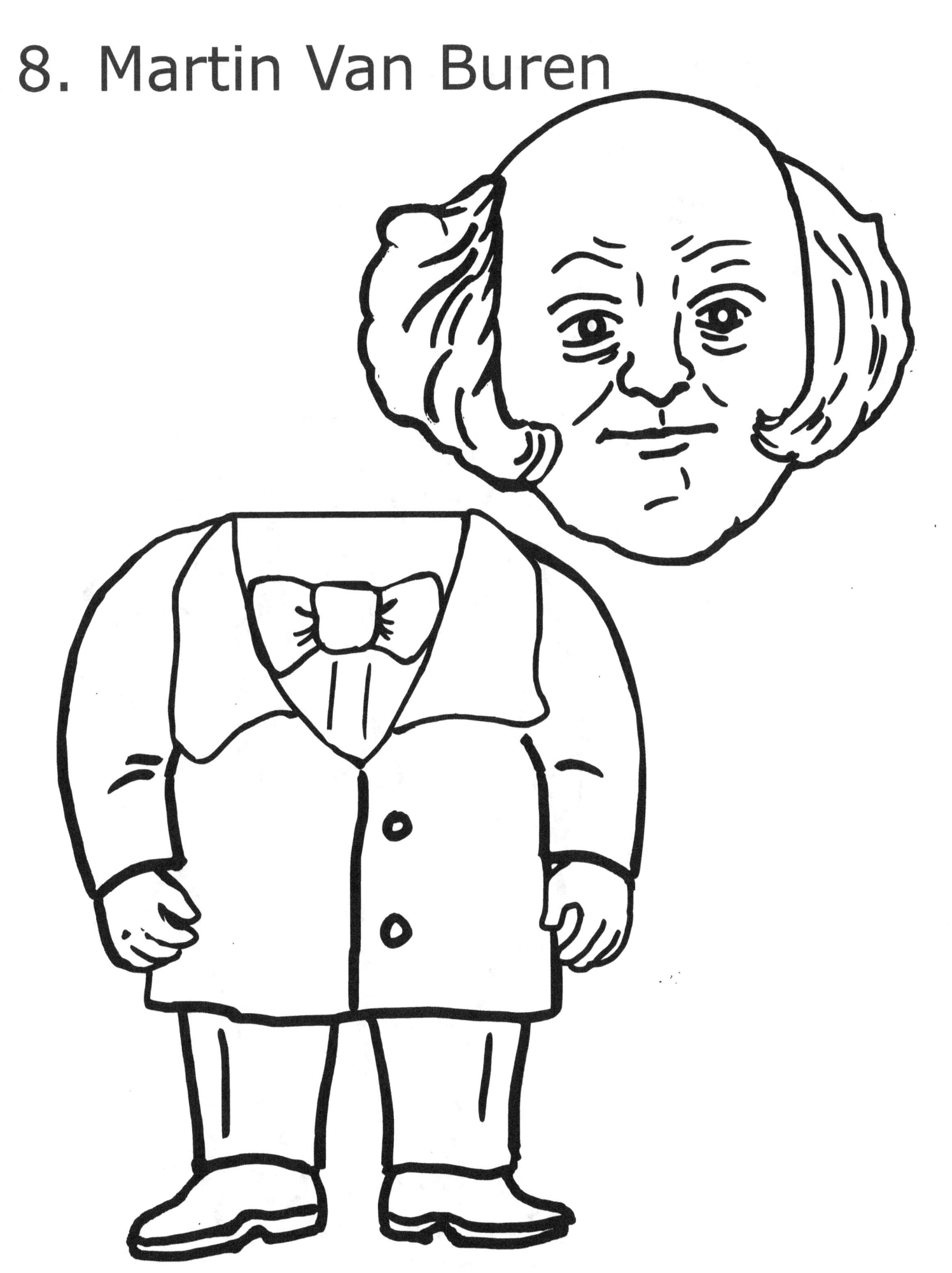

9. William Henry Harrison

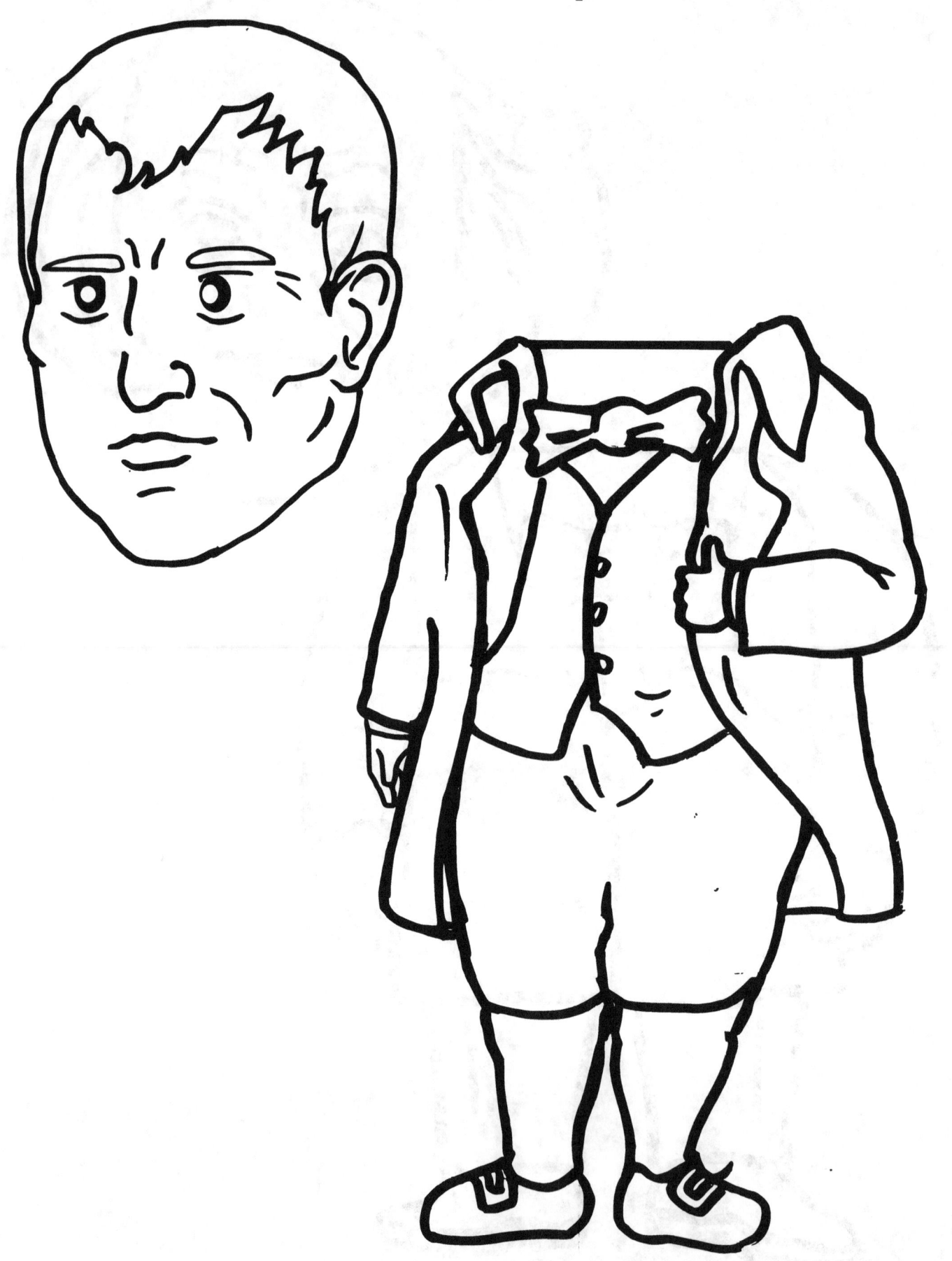

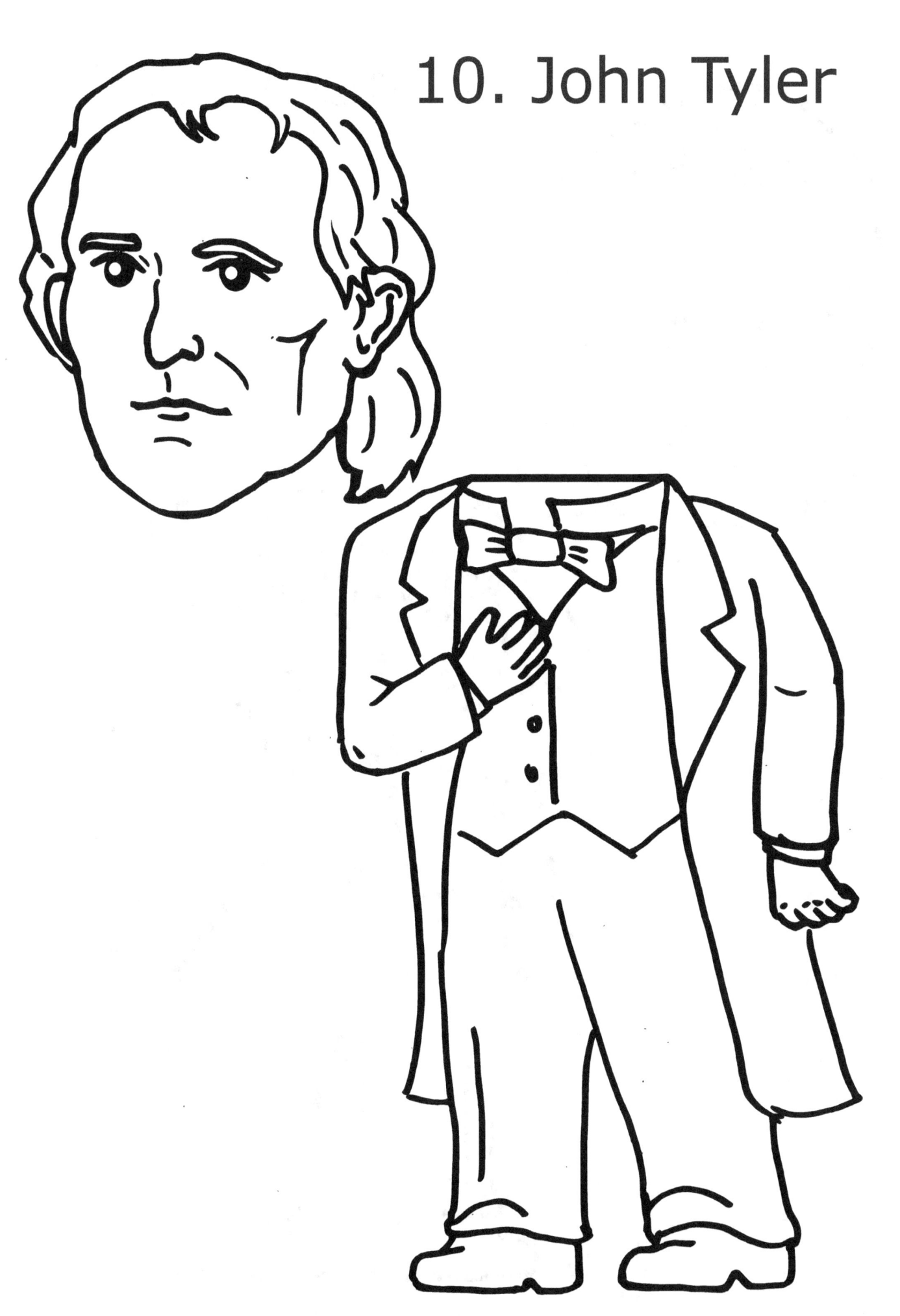

10. John Tyler

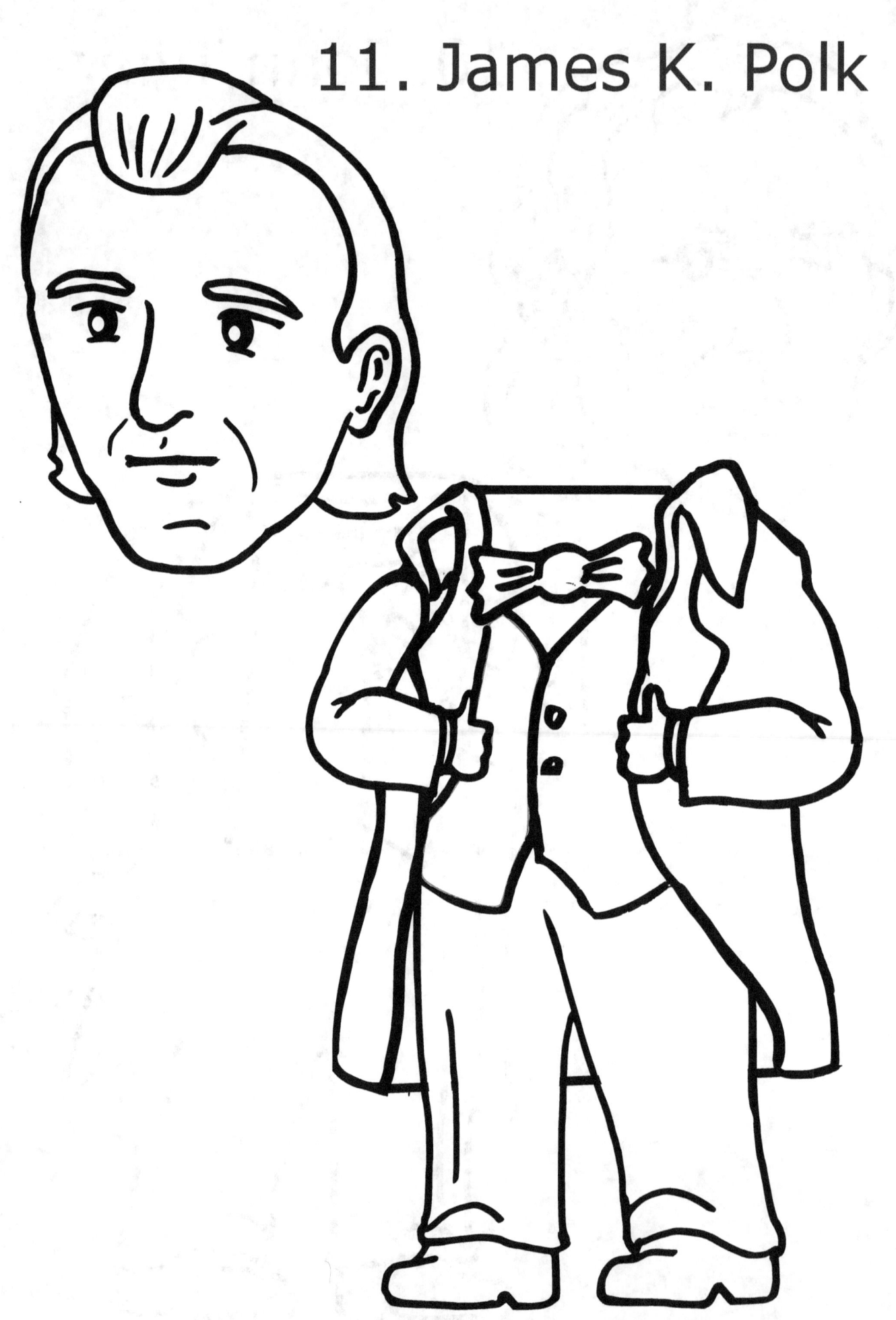

12. Zachary Taylor

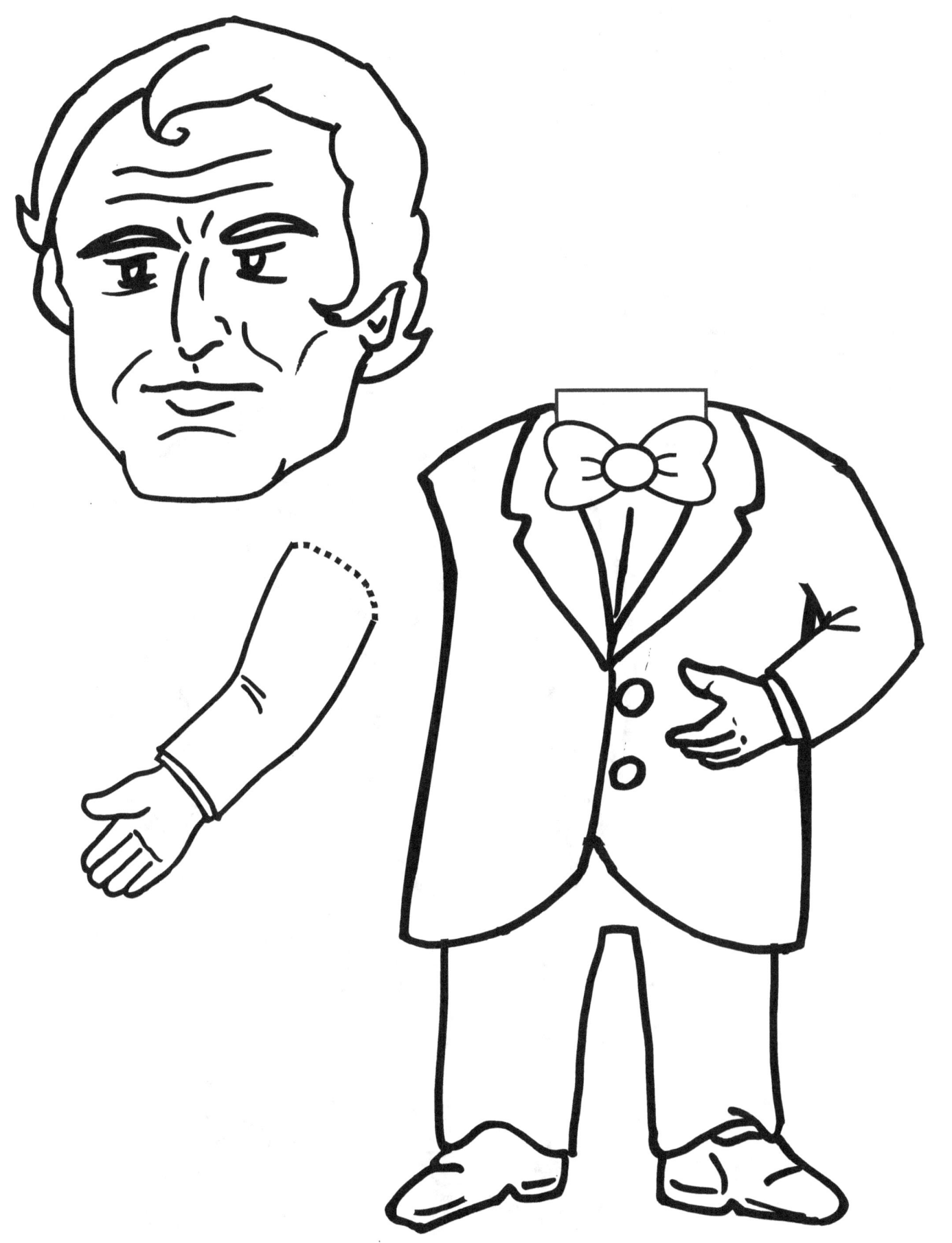

13. Millard Fillmore

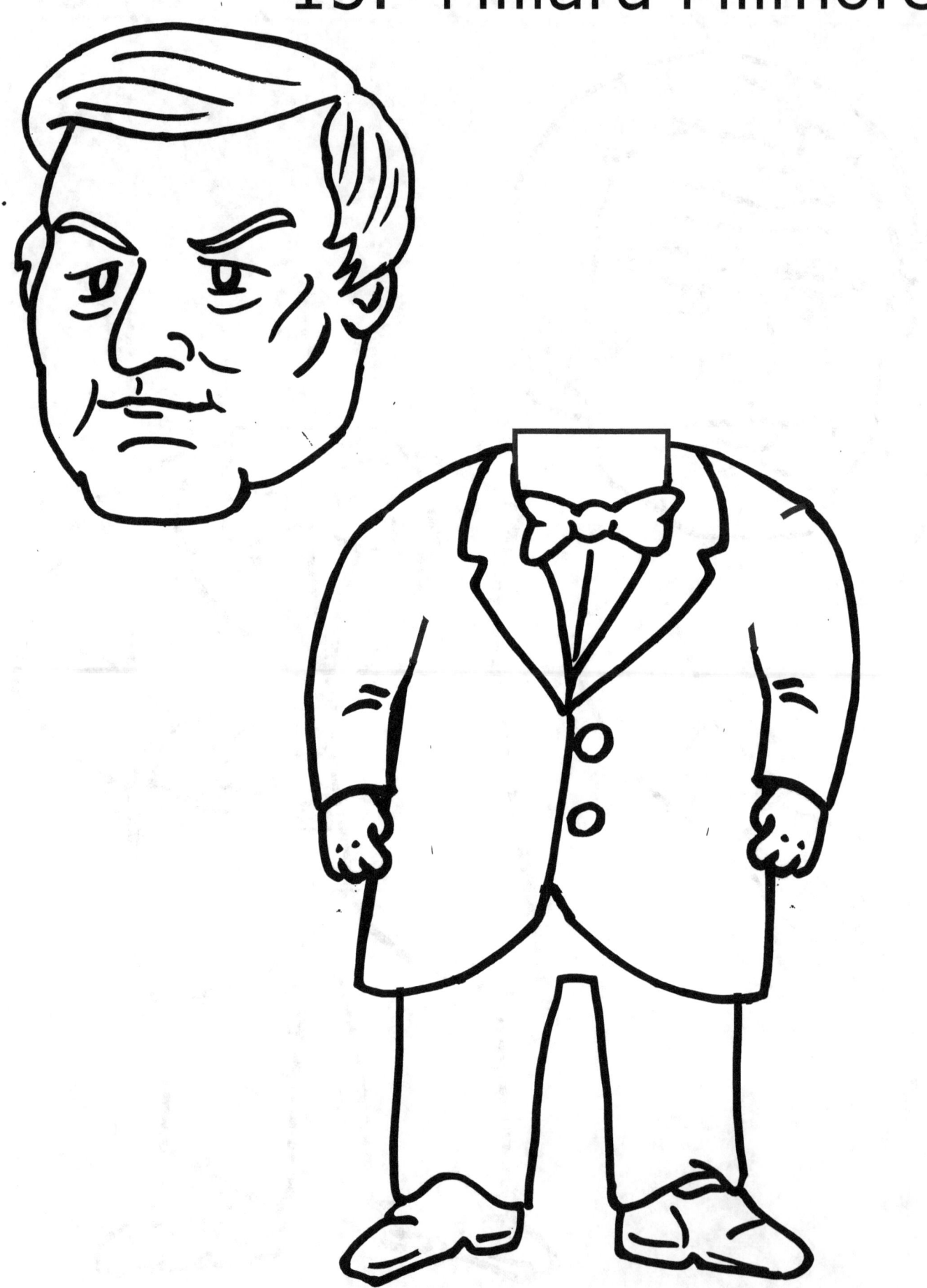

14. Franklin Pierce

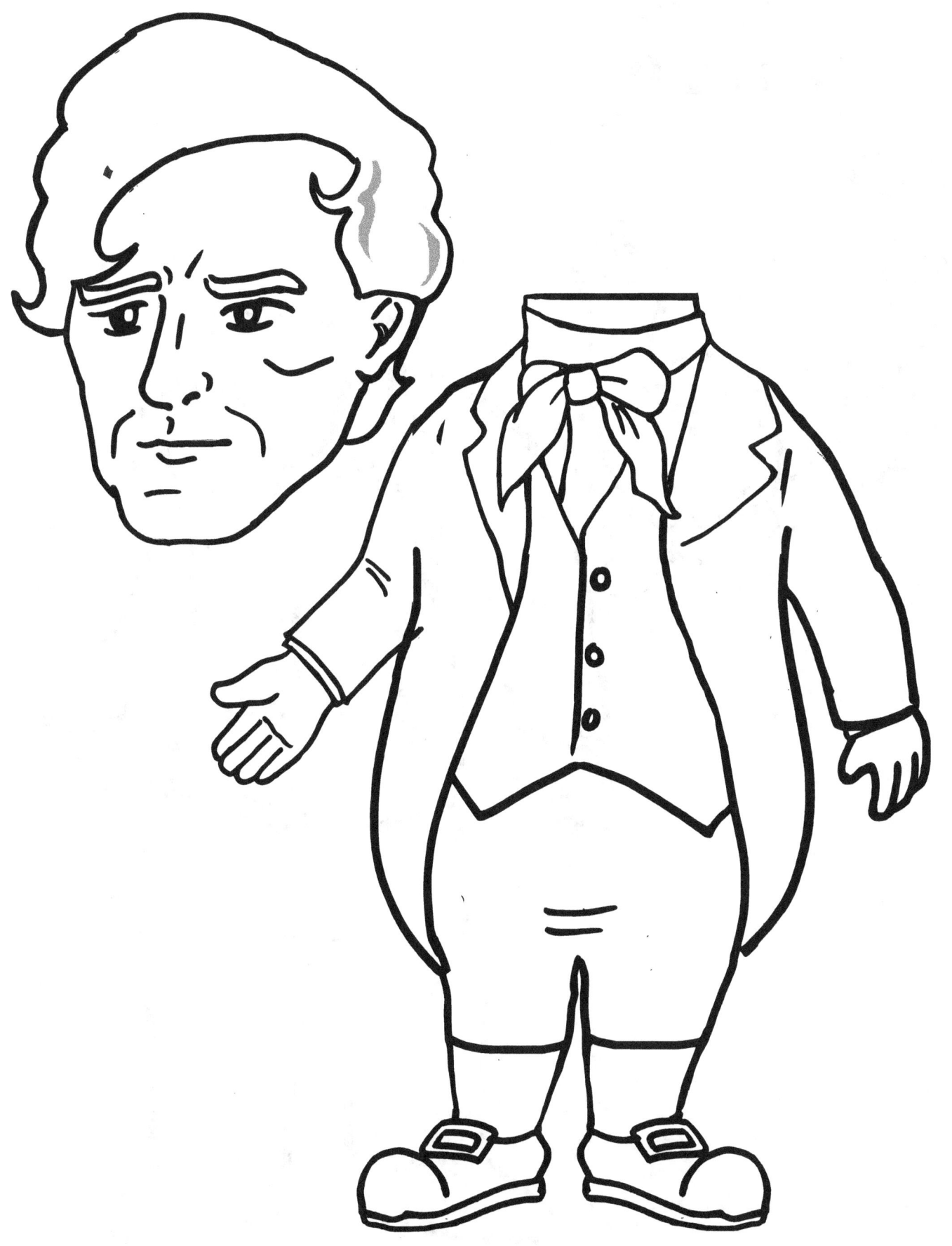

15. James Buchanan

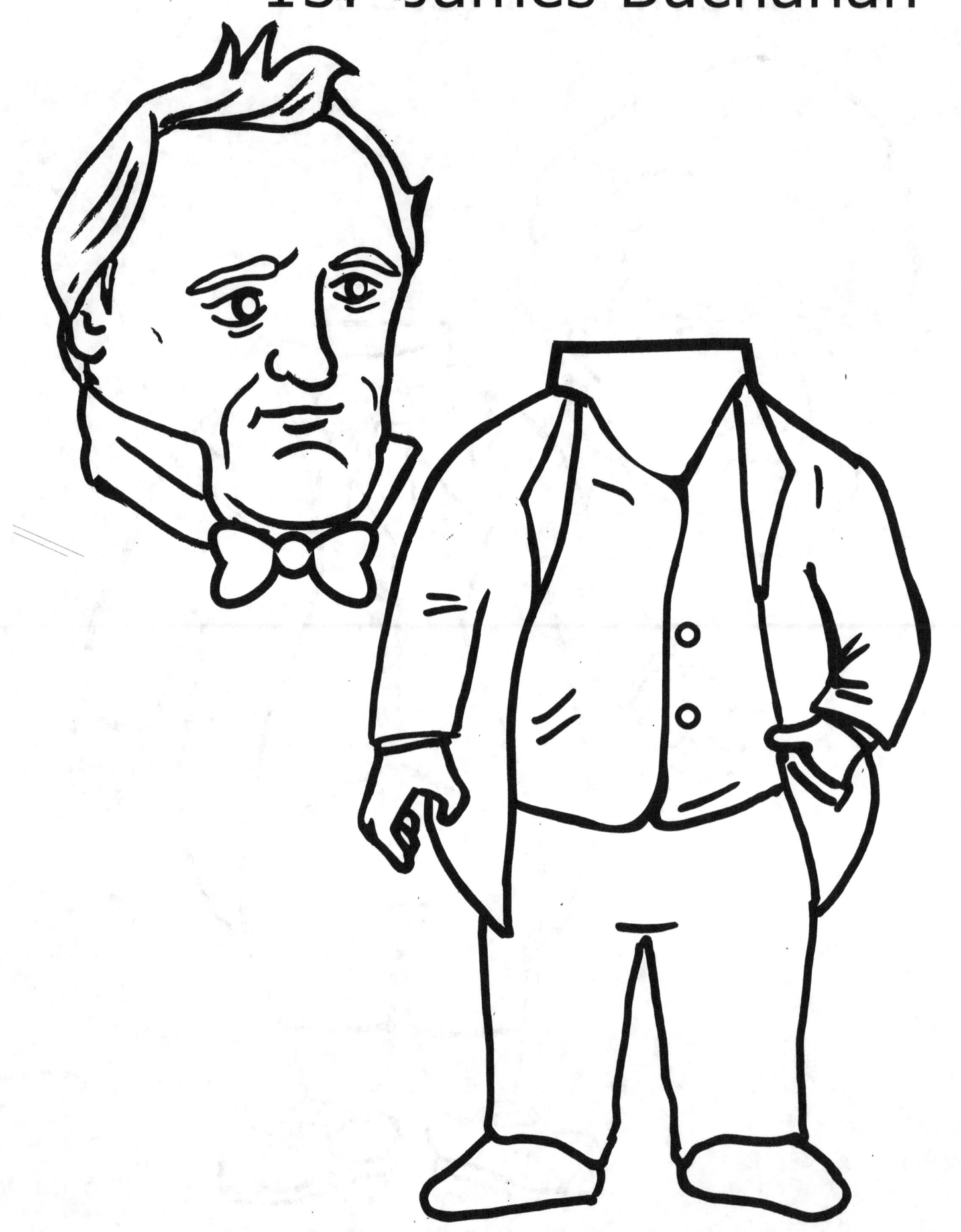

16. Abraham Lincoln

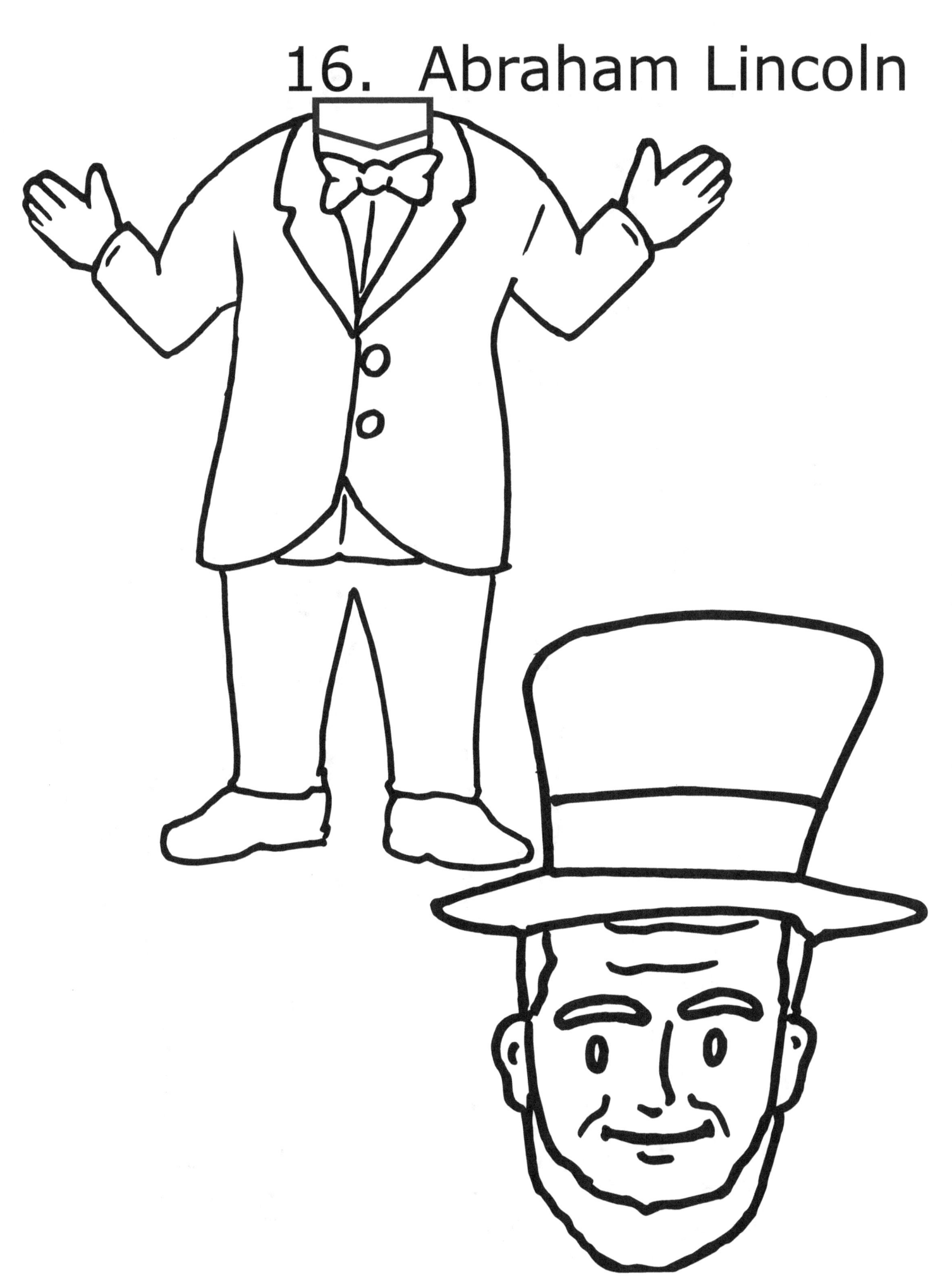

17. Andrew Johnson

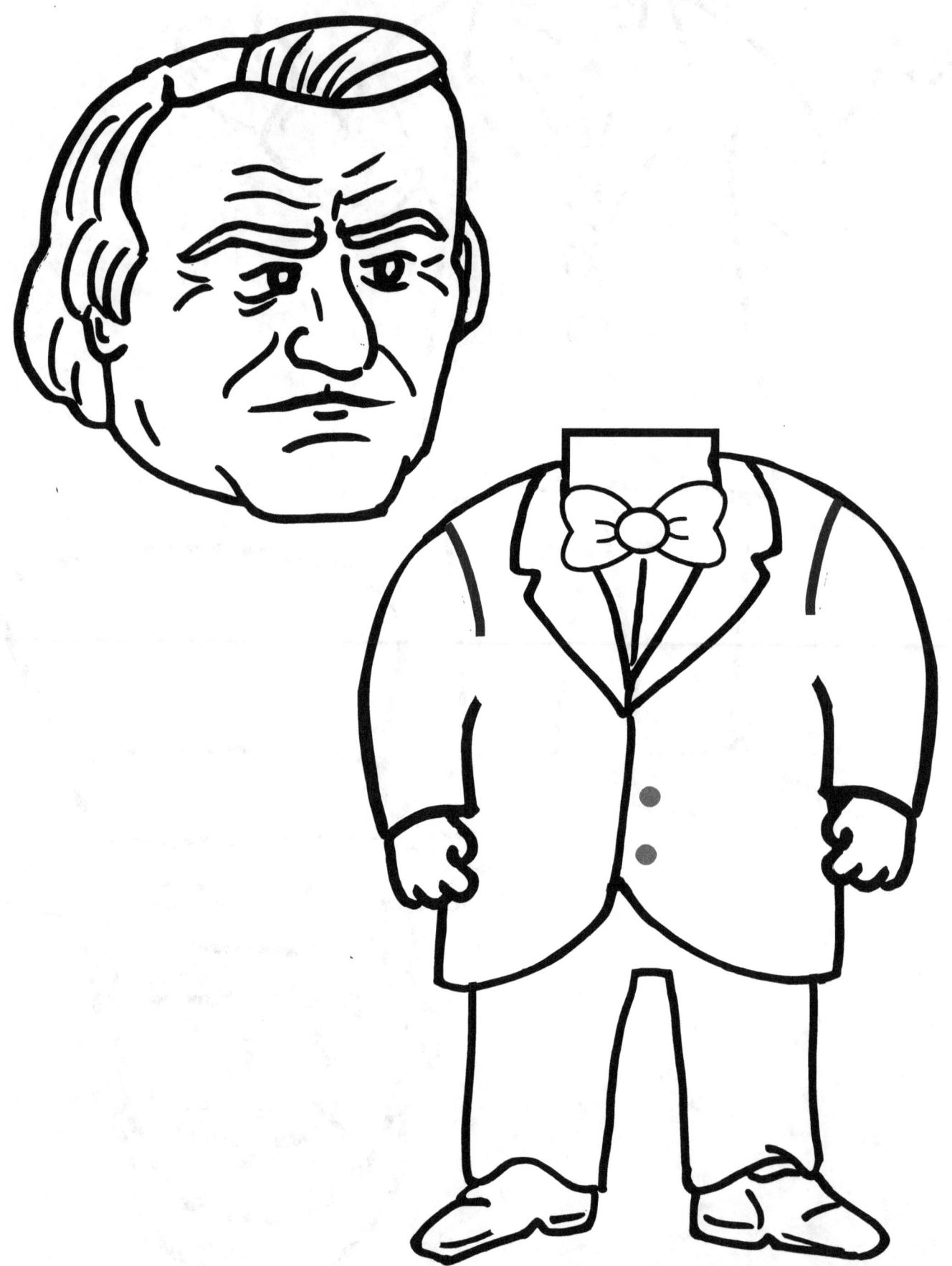

18. Ulysses S. Grant

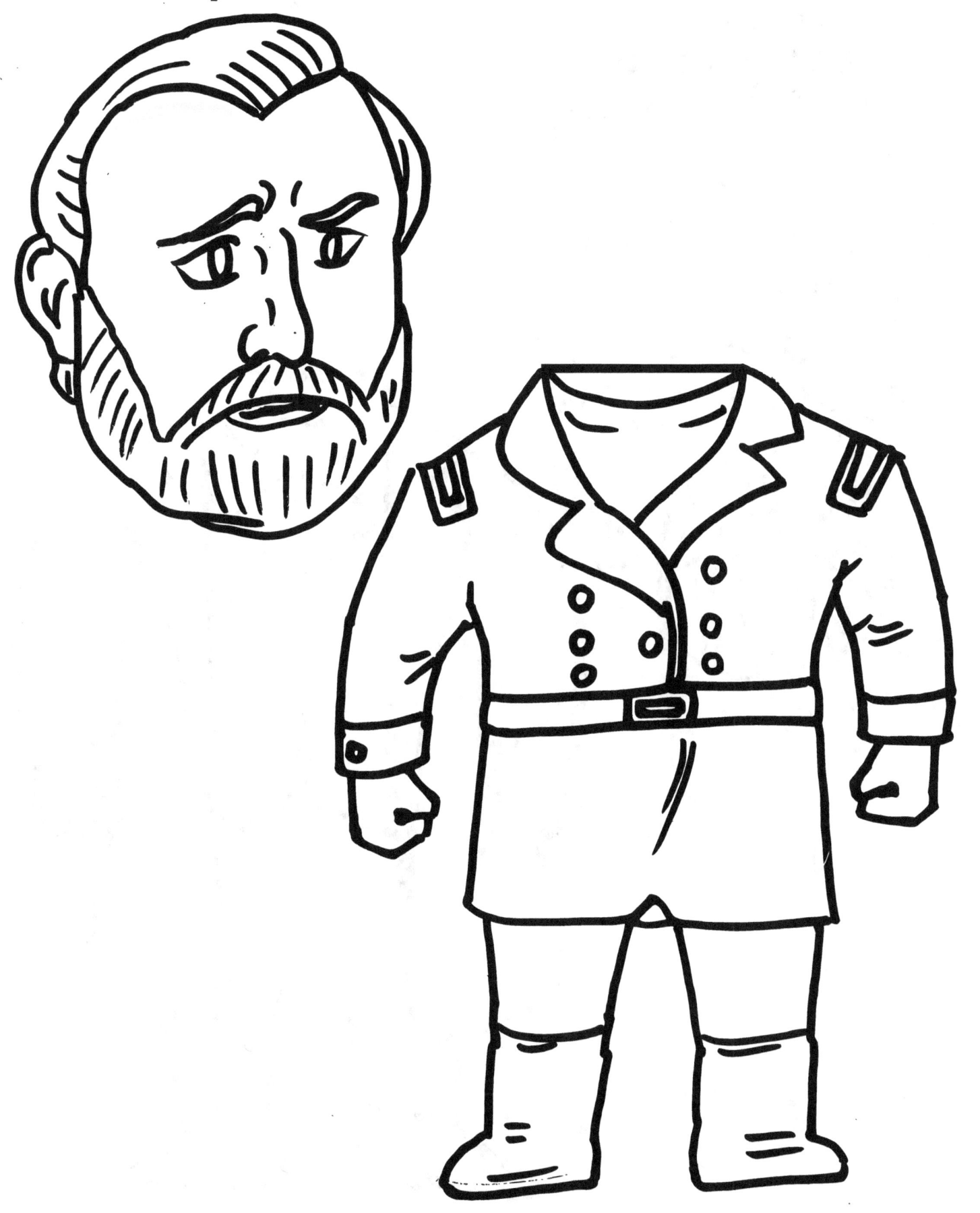

19. Rutherford B. Hayes

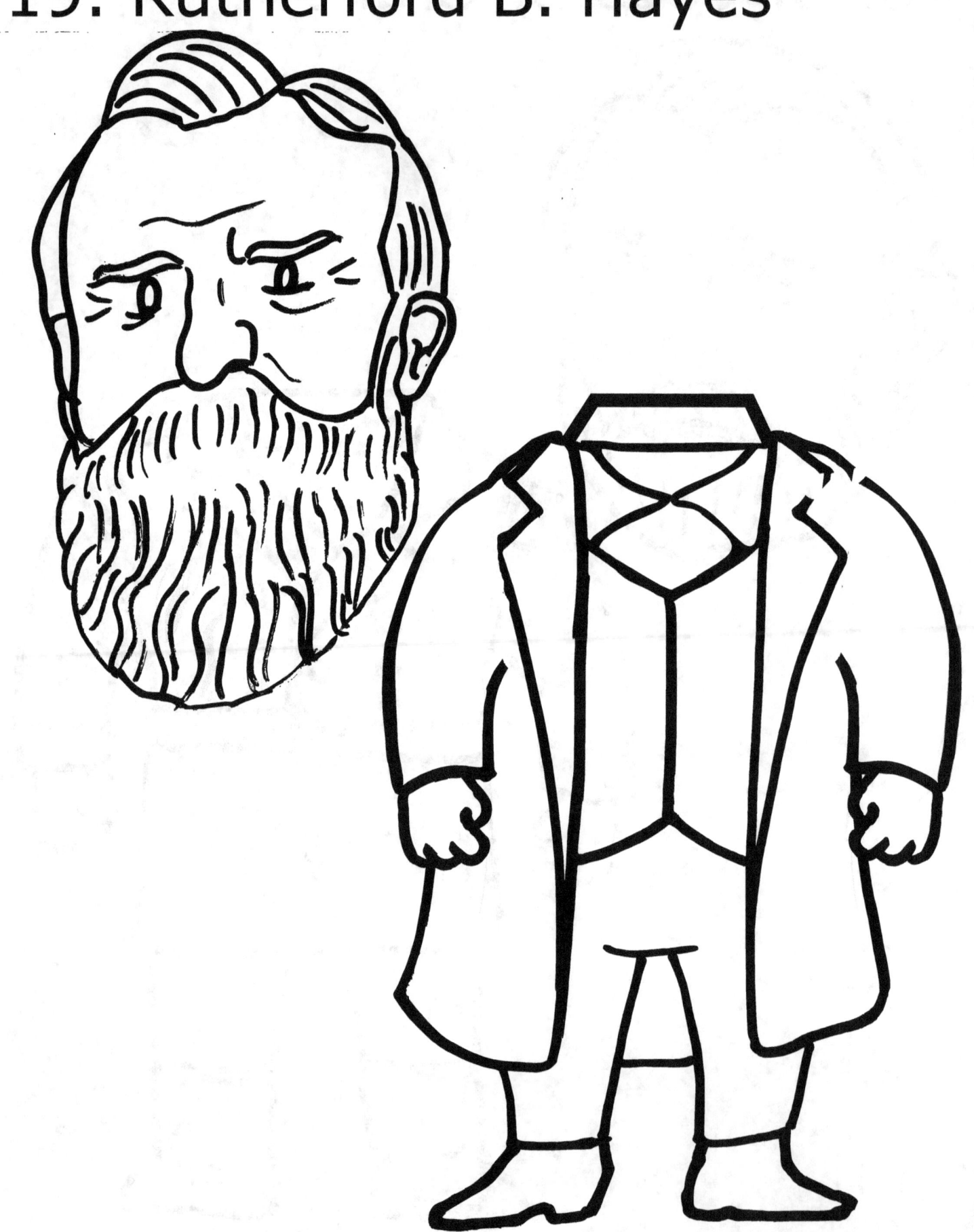

20. James A. Garfield

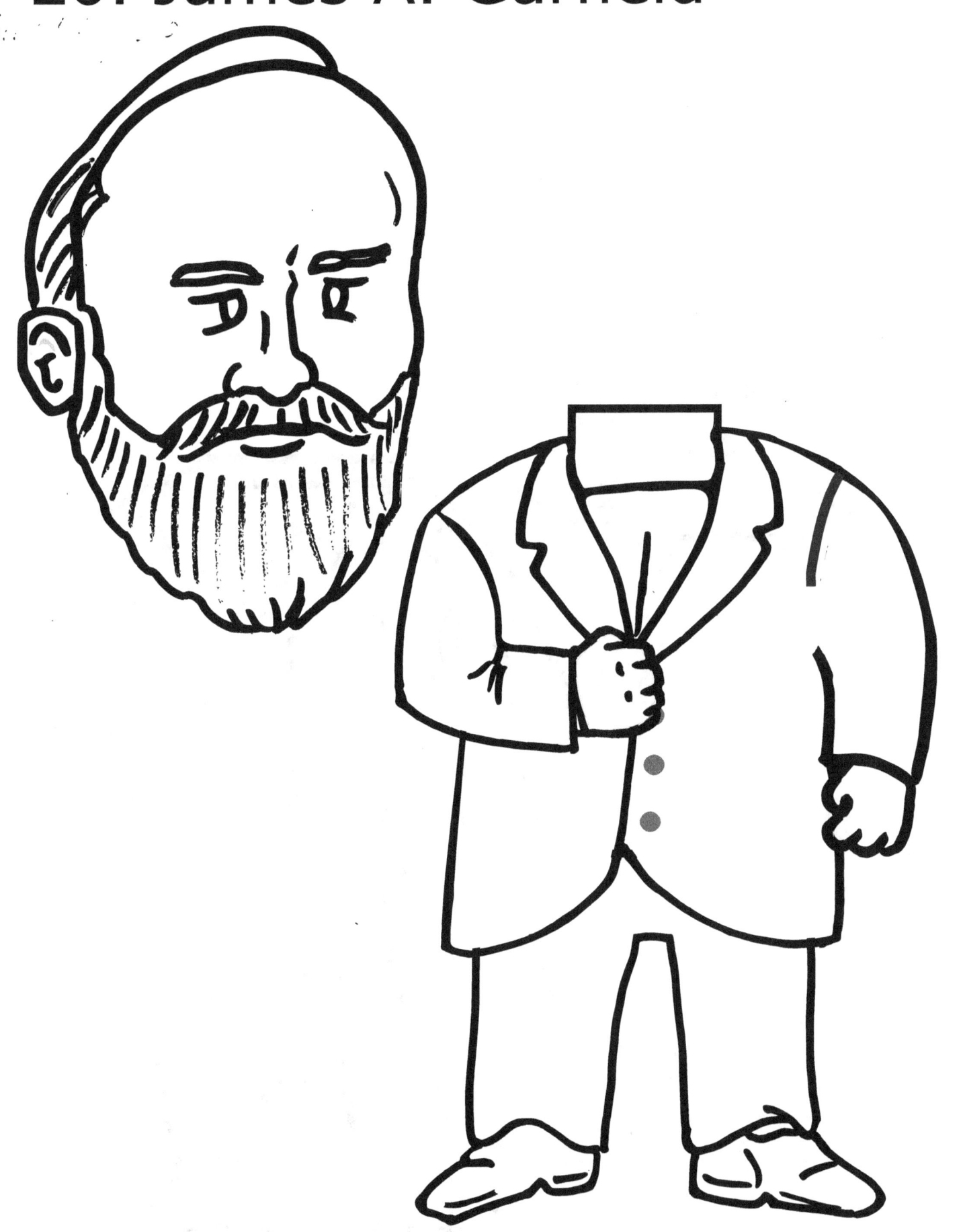

21. Chester A. Arthur

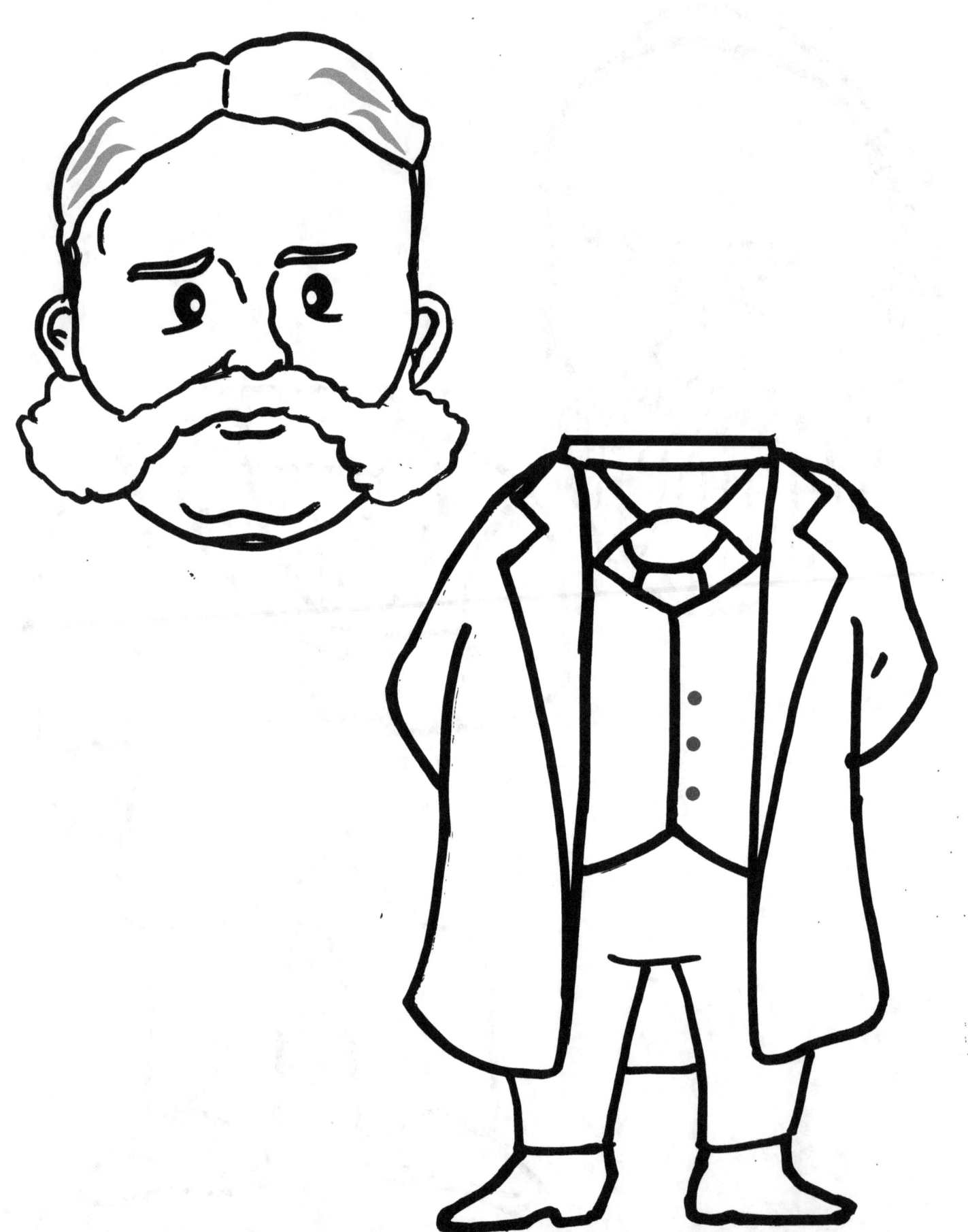

22+24: Glover Cleveland

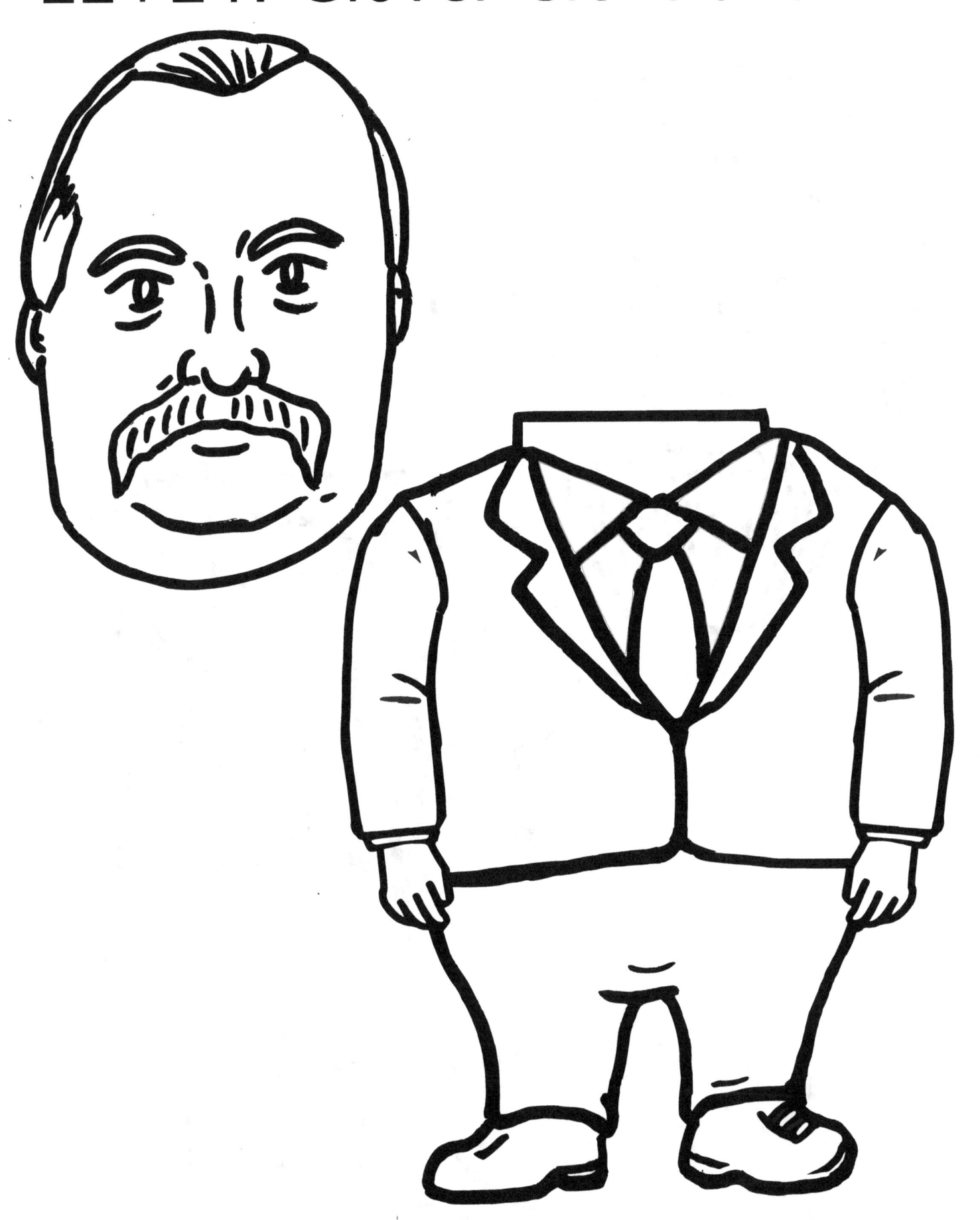

23. Benjamin Harrison

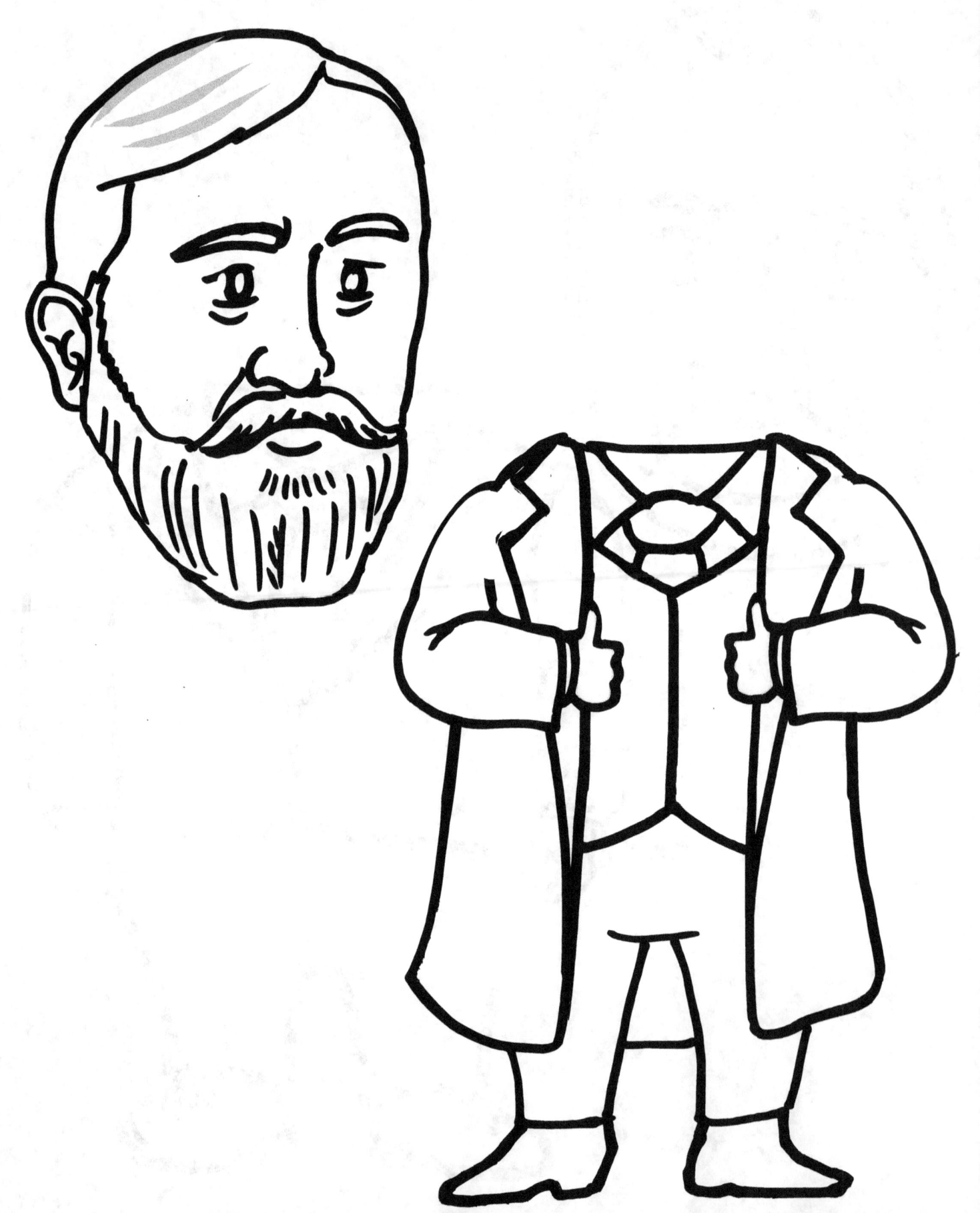

25. William Mckinley

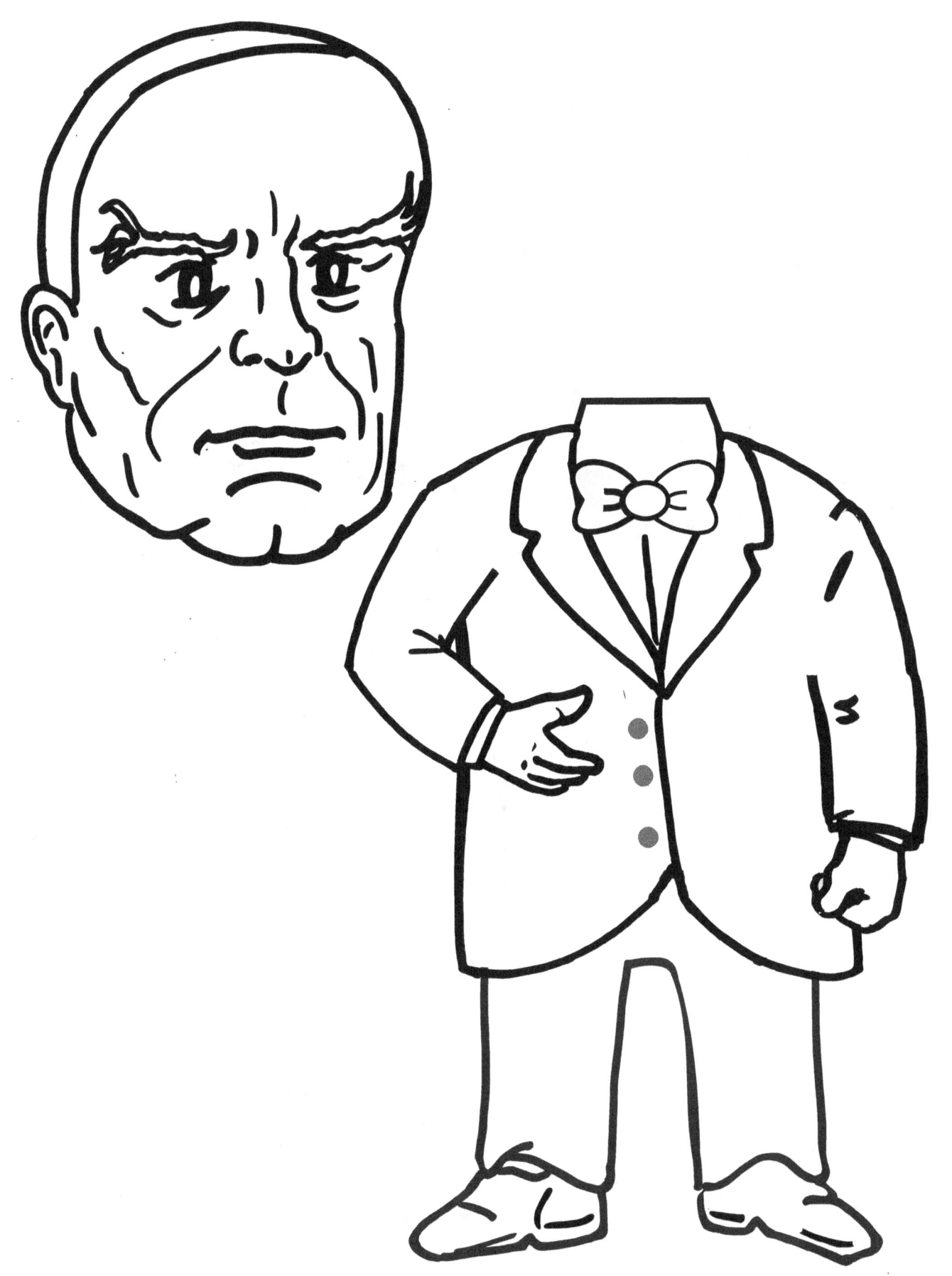

26. Theodore Roosevelt

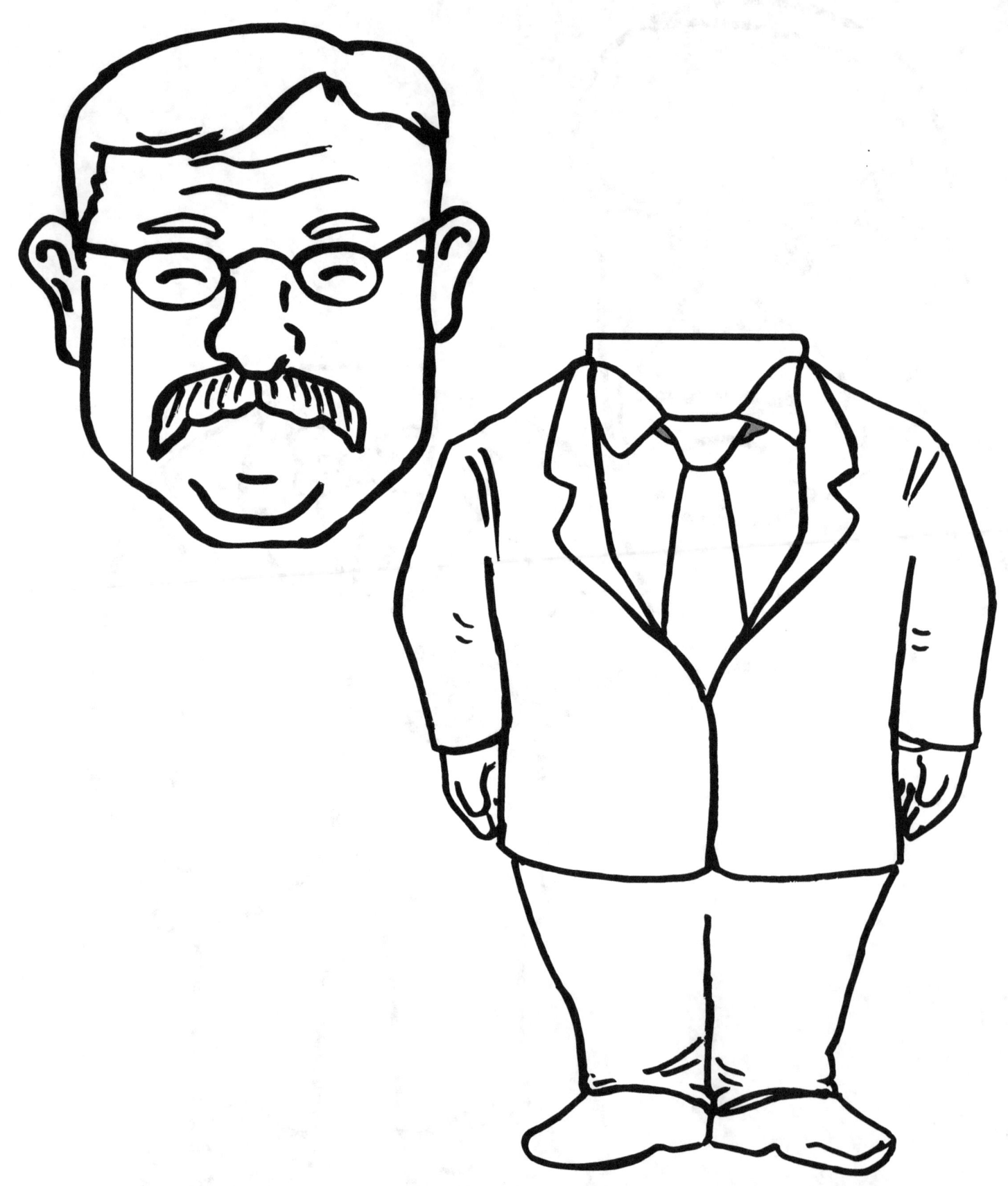

27. William Howard Taft

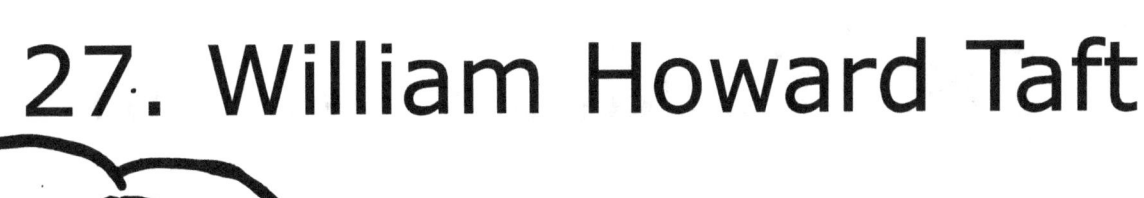

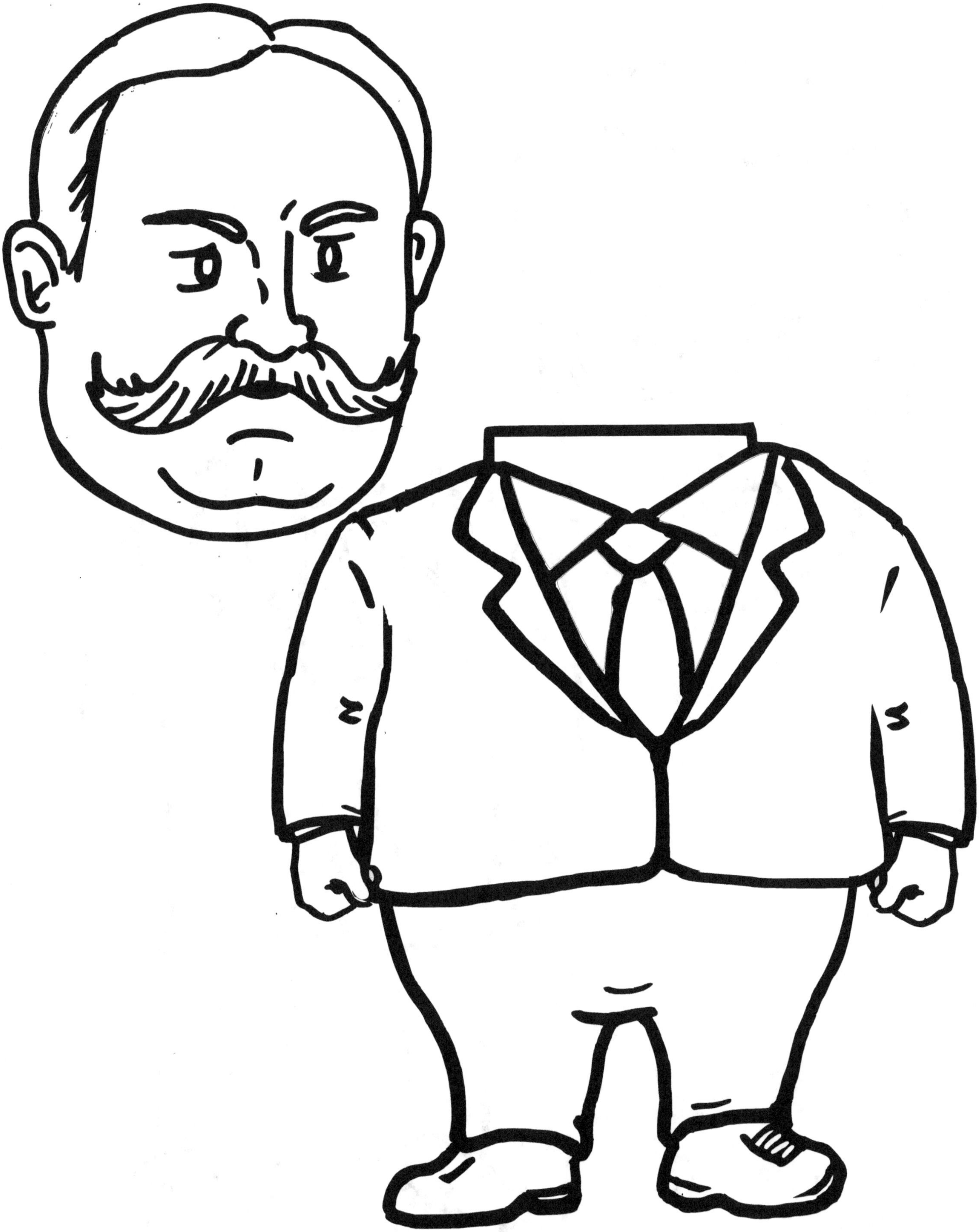

28. Woodrow Wilson

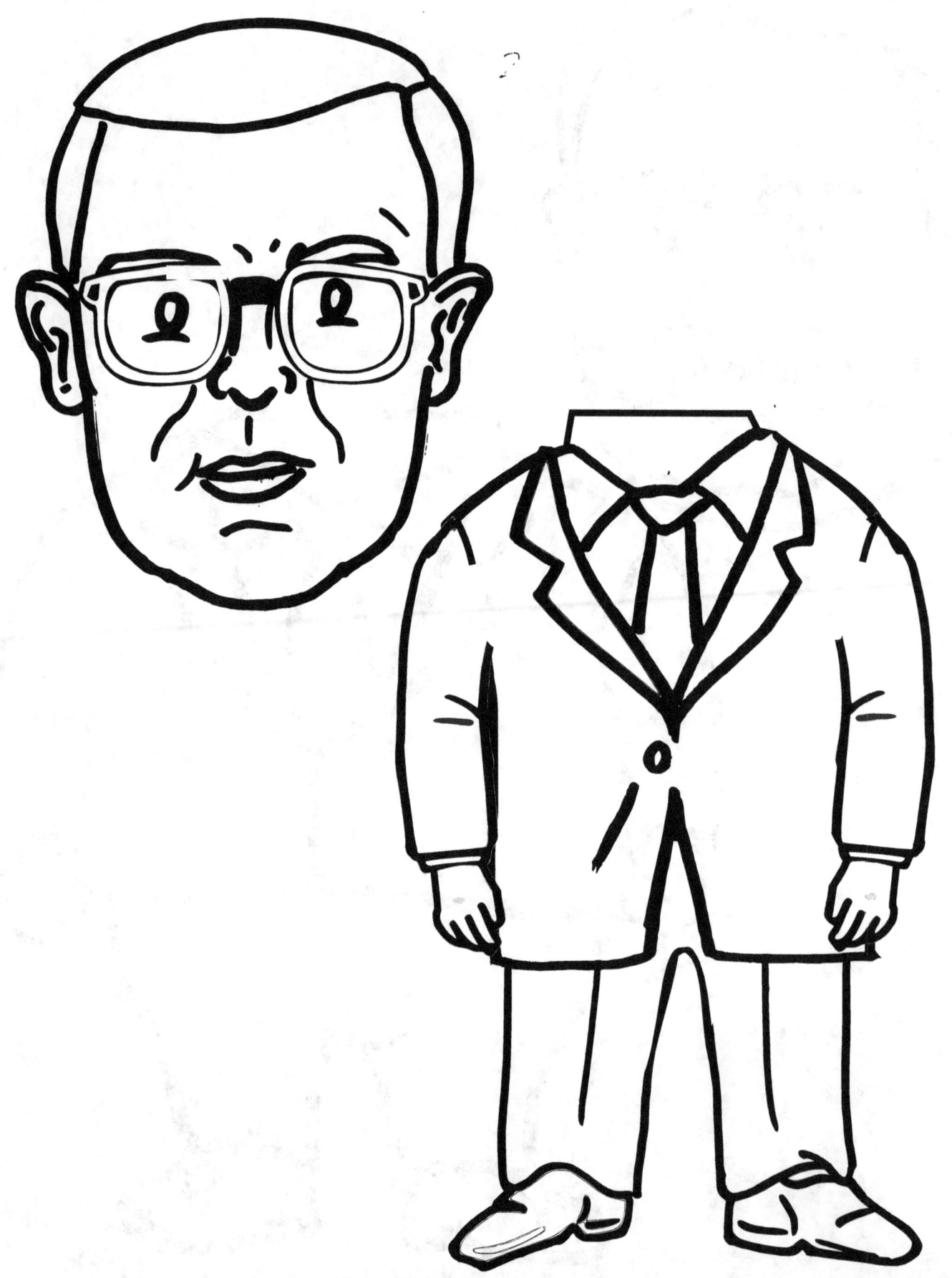

29. Warren G. Harding

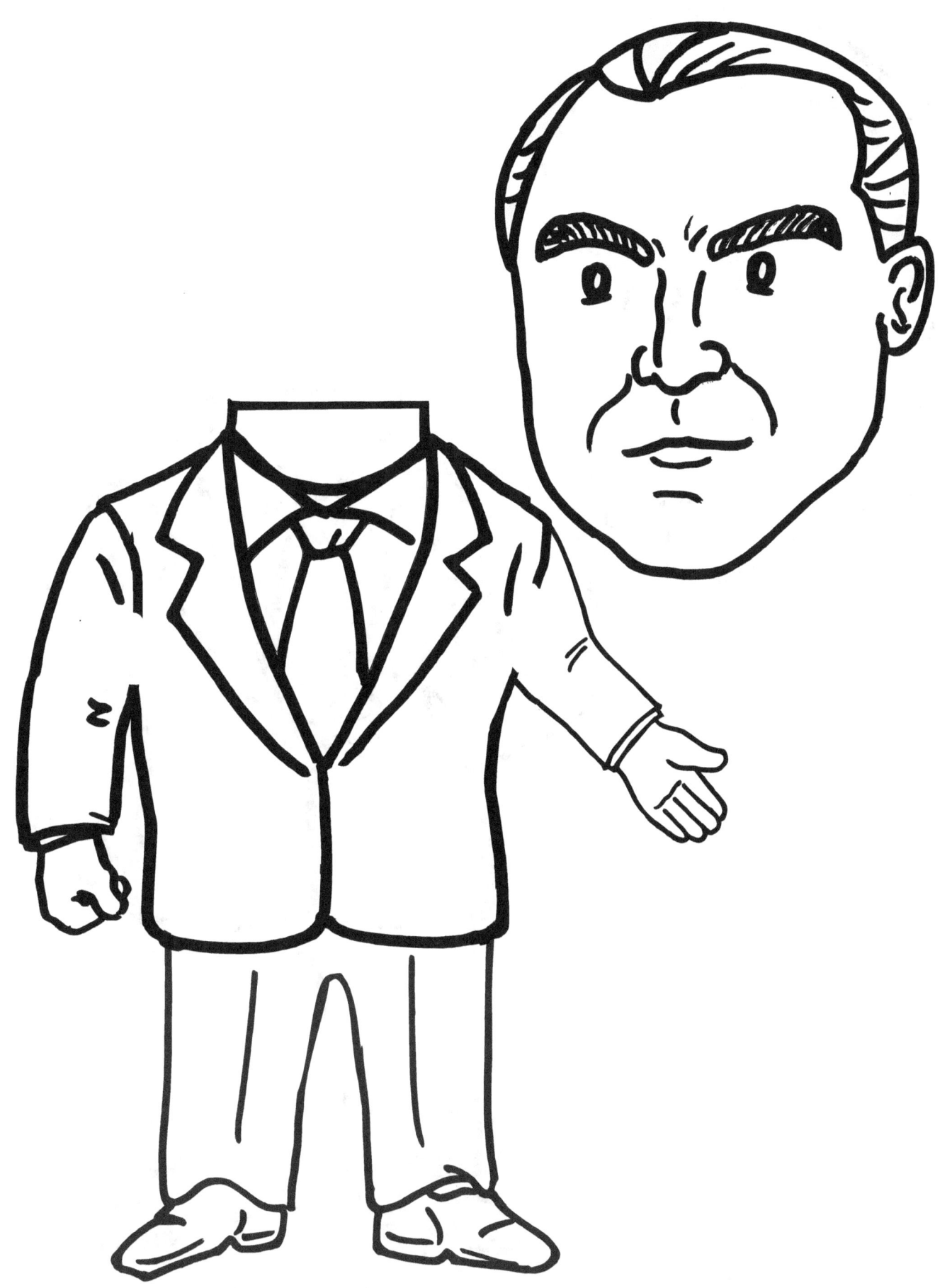

30 Calvin Coolidge

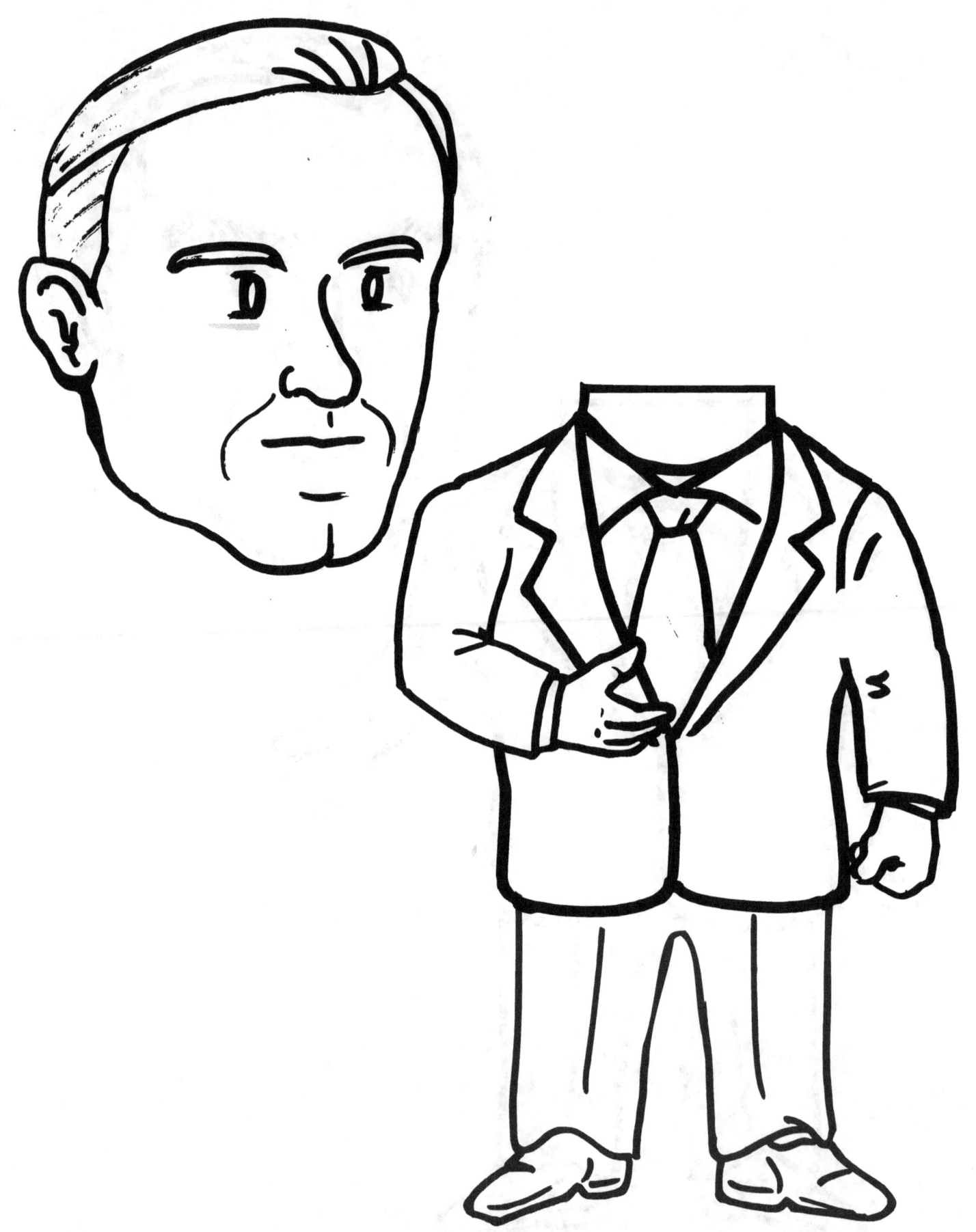

31. Herbert Hoover

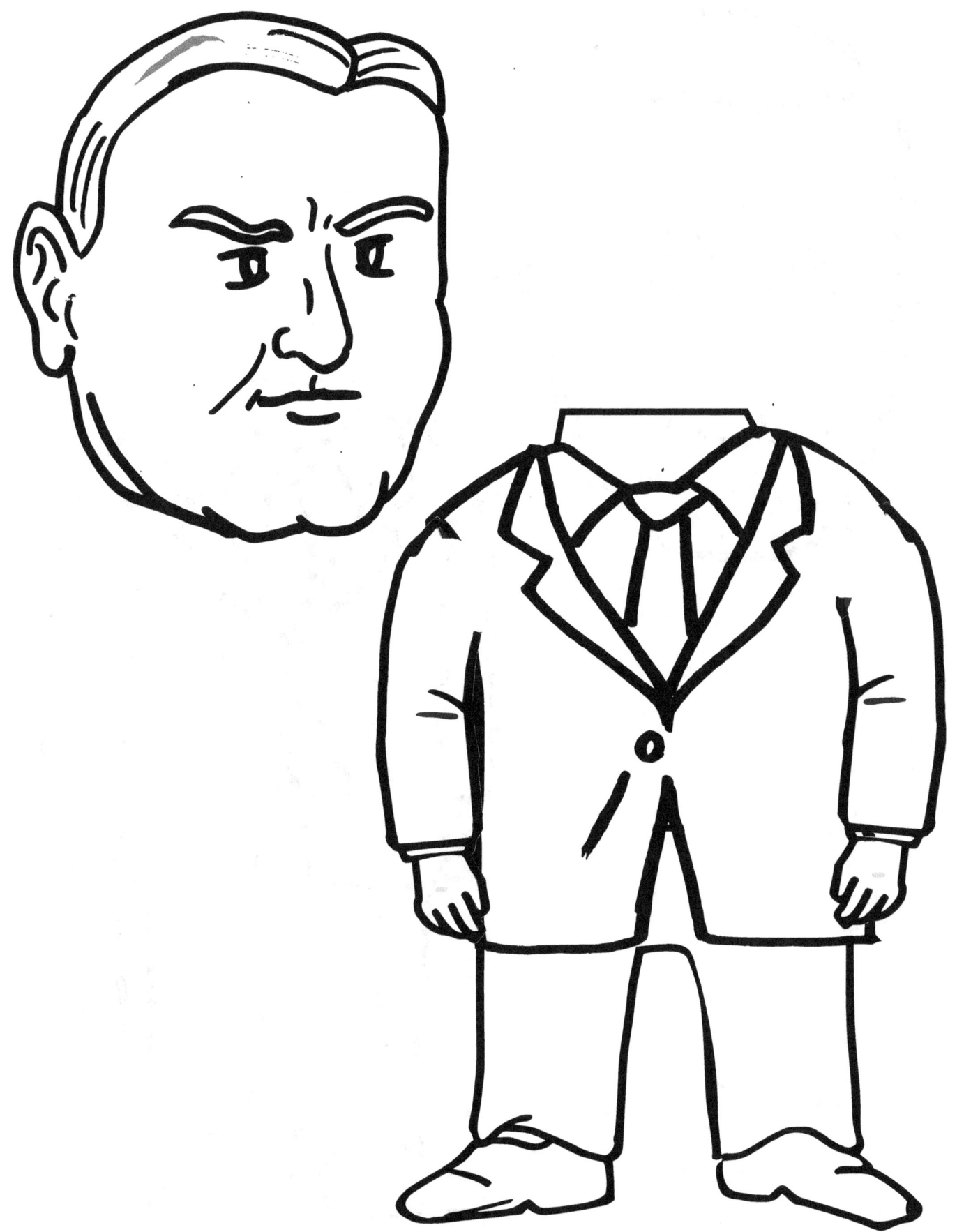

32. Franklin D. Roosevelt

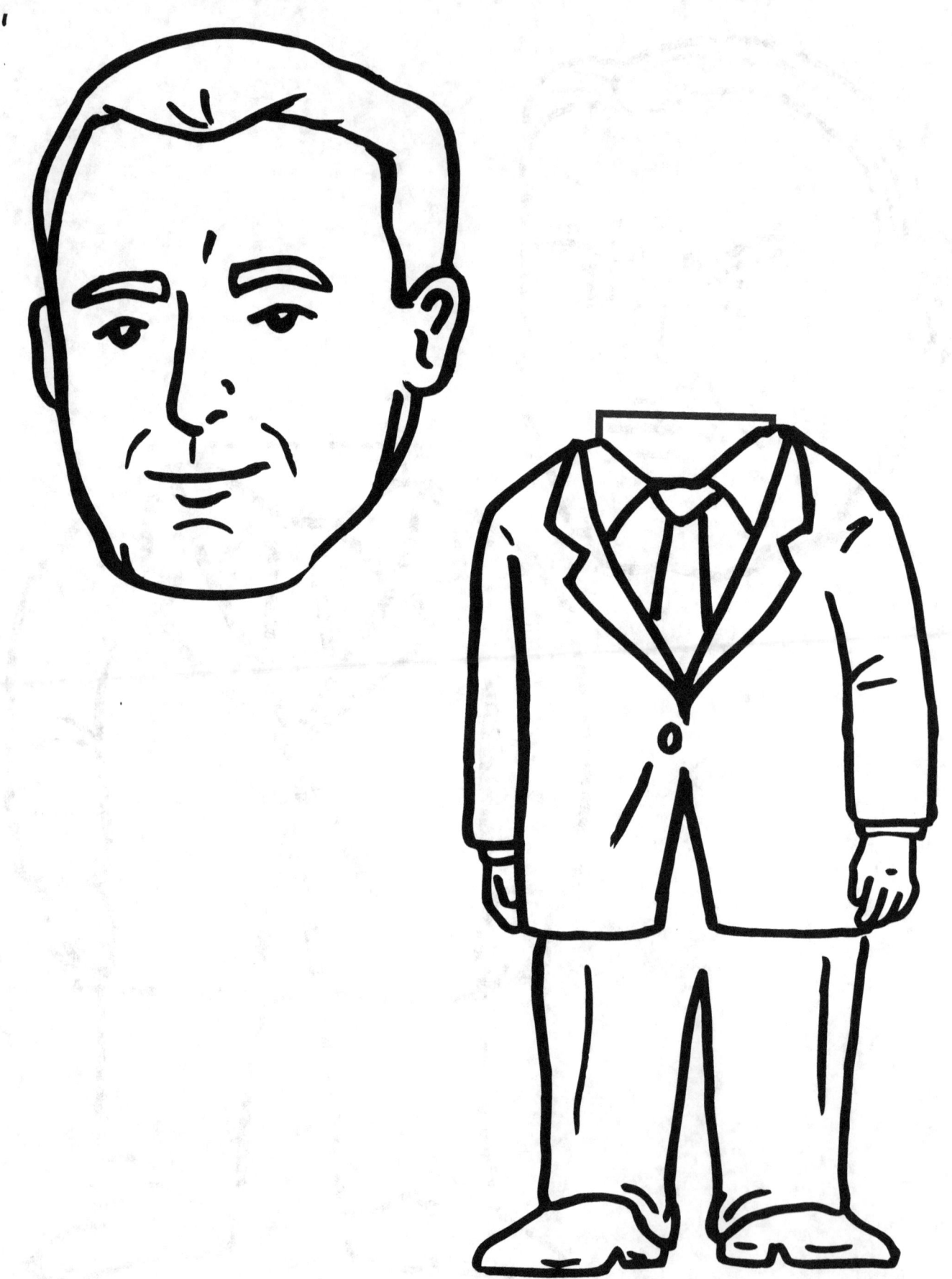

33. Harry S. Truman

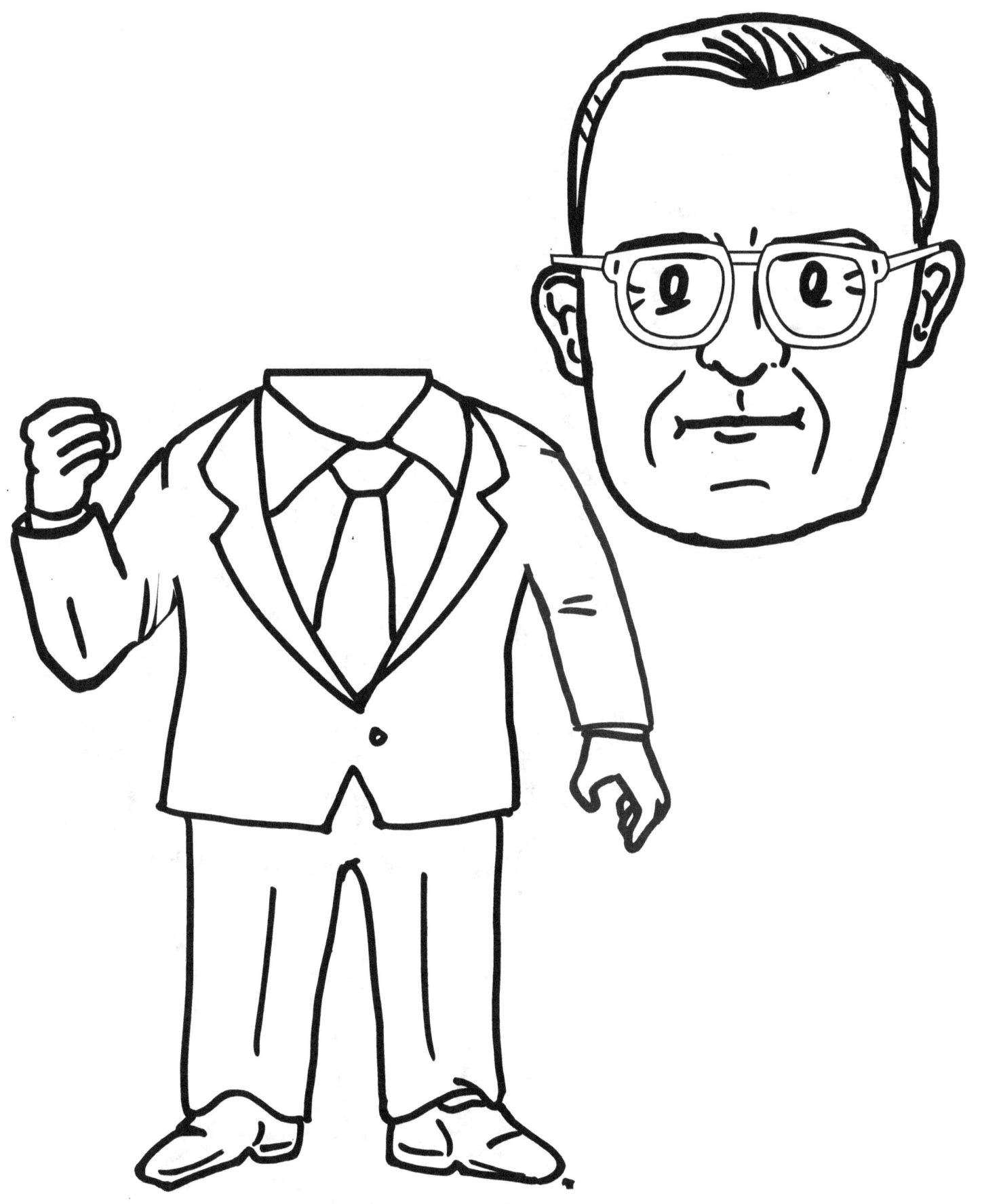

34. Dwight D. Eisenhower

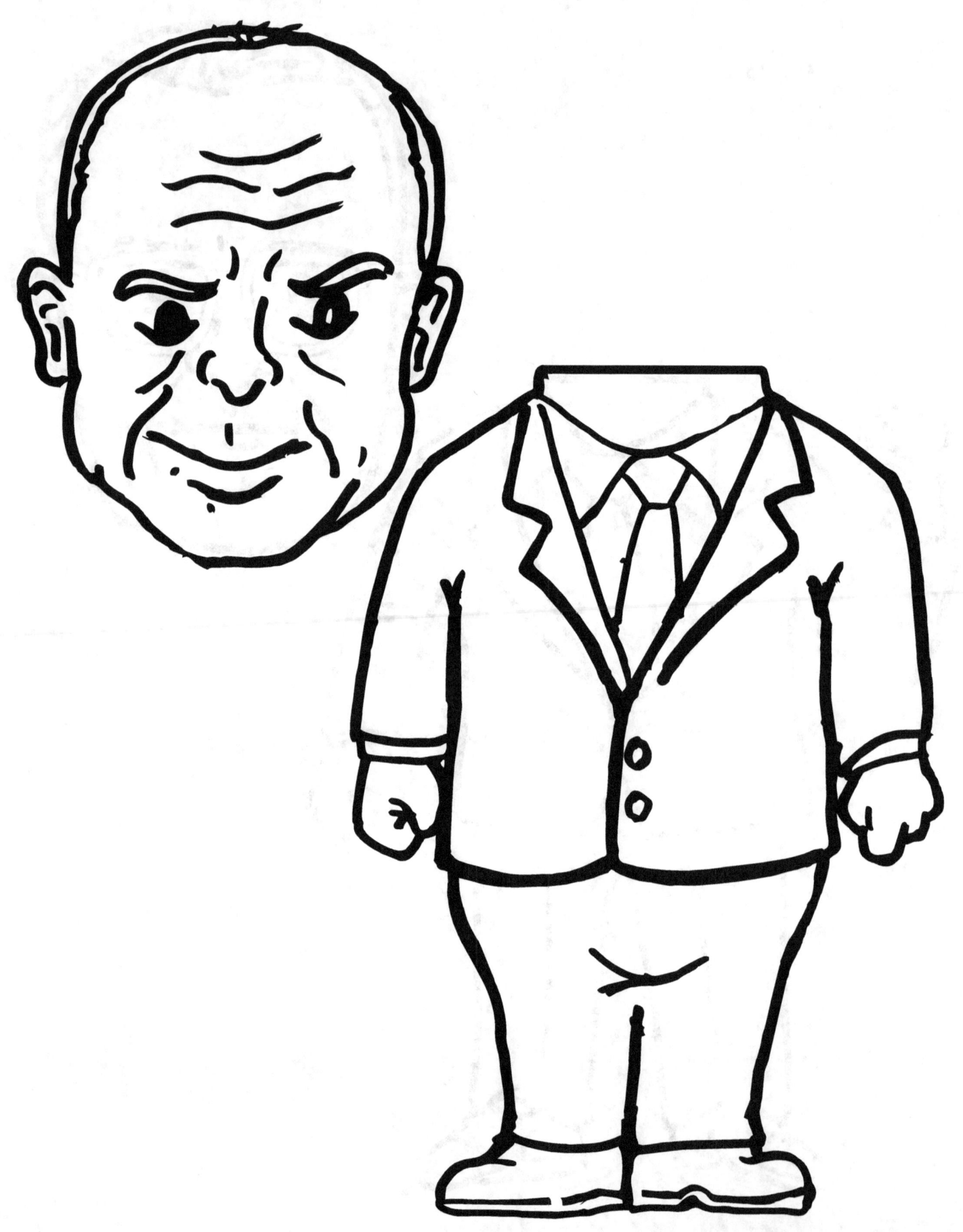

36. Lyndon B. Johnson

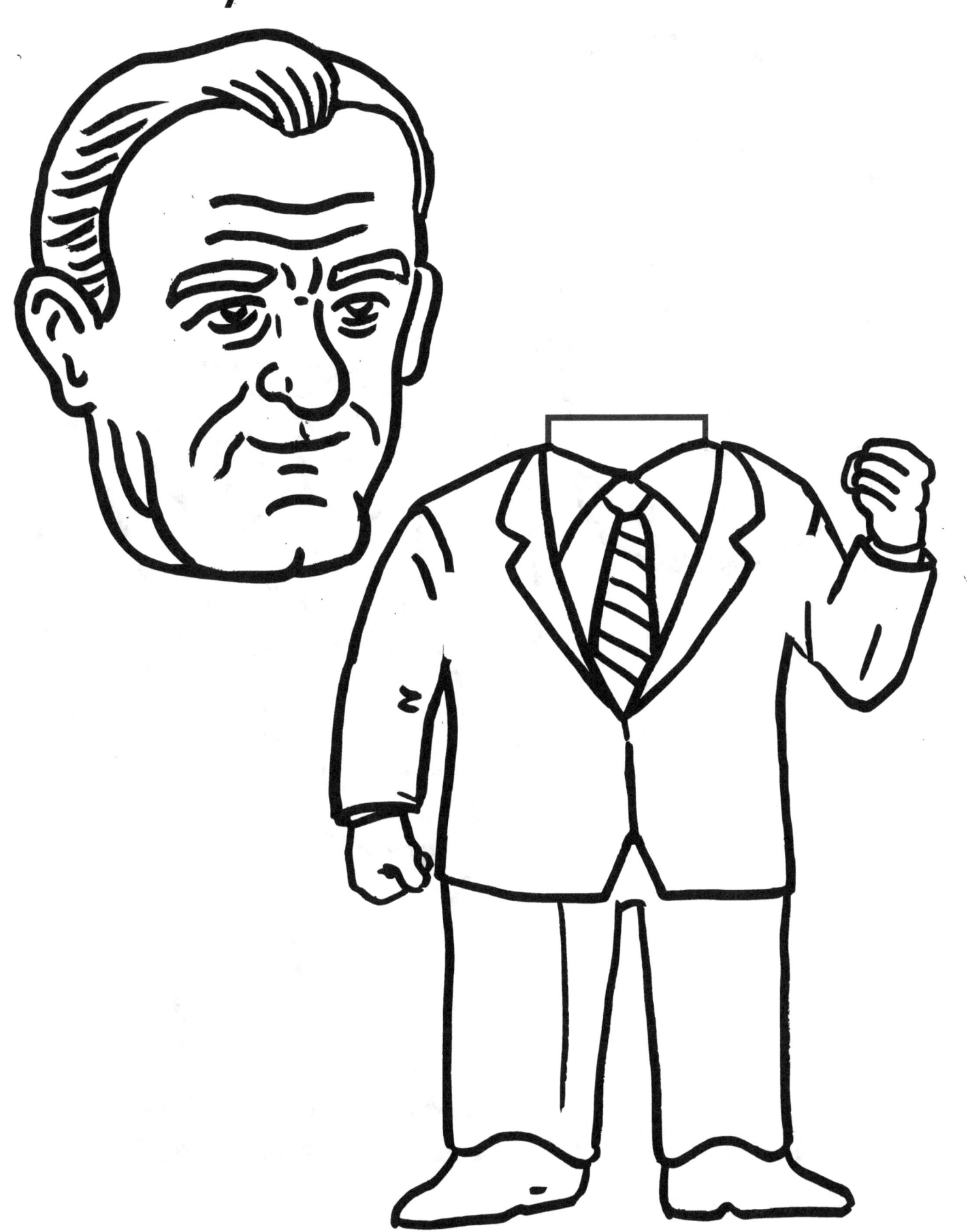

37. Richard Nixon

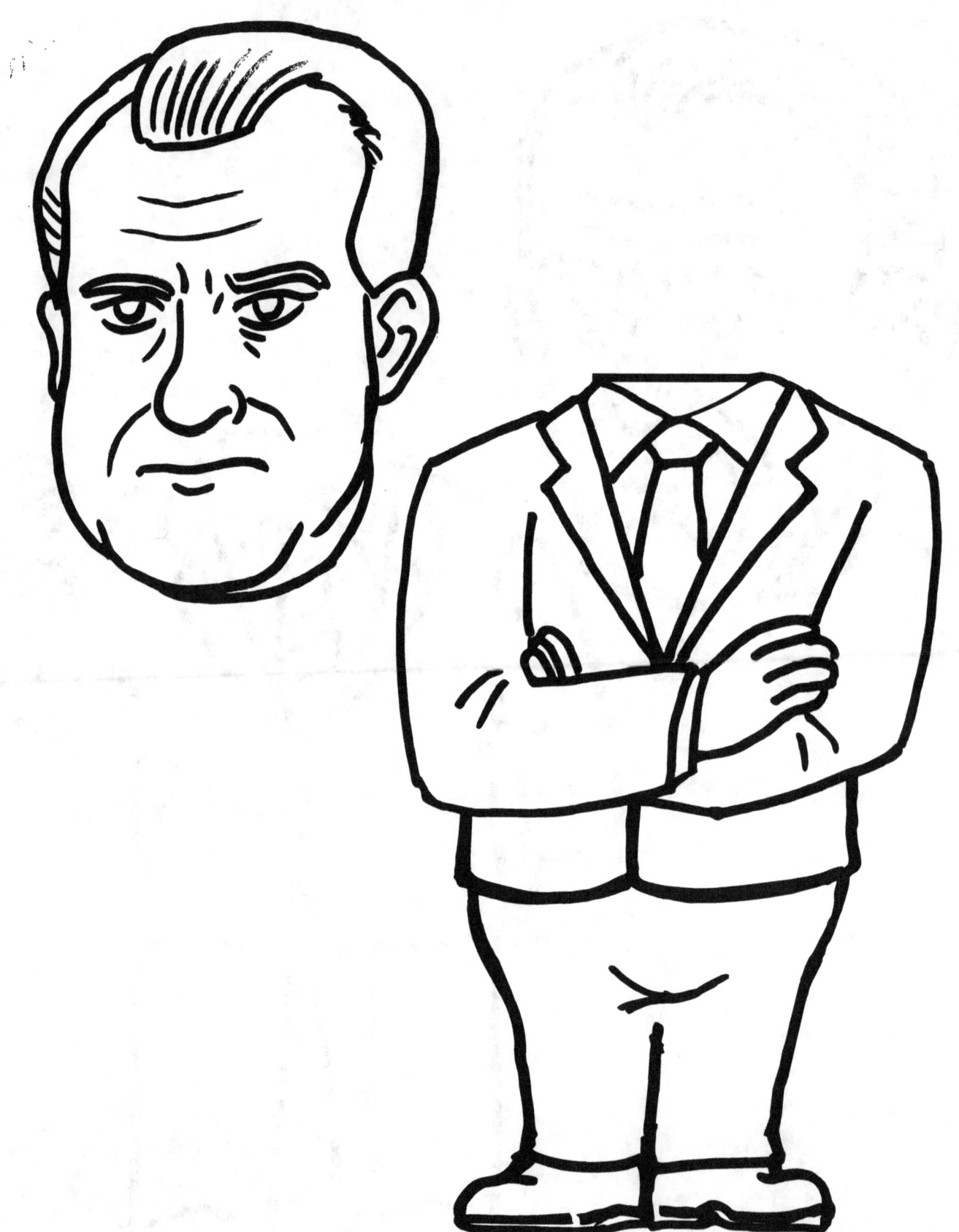

35. John F. Kennedy

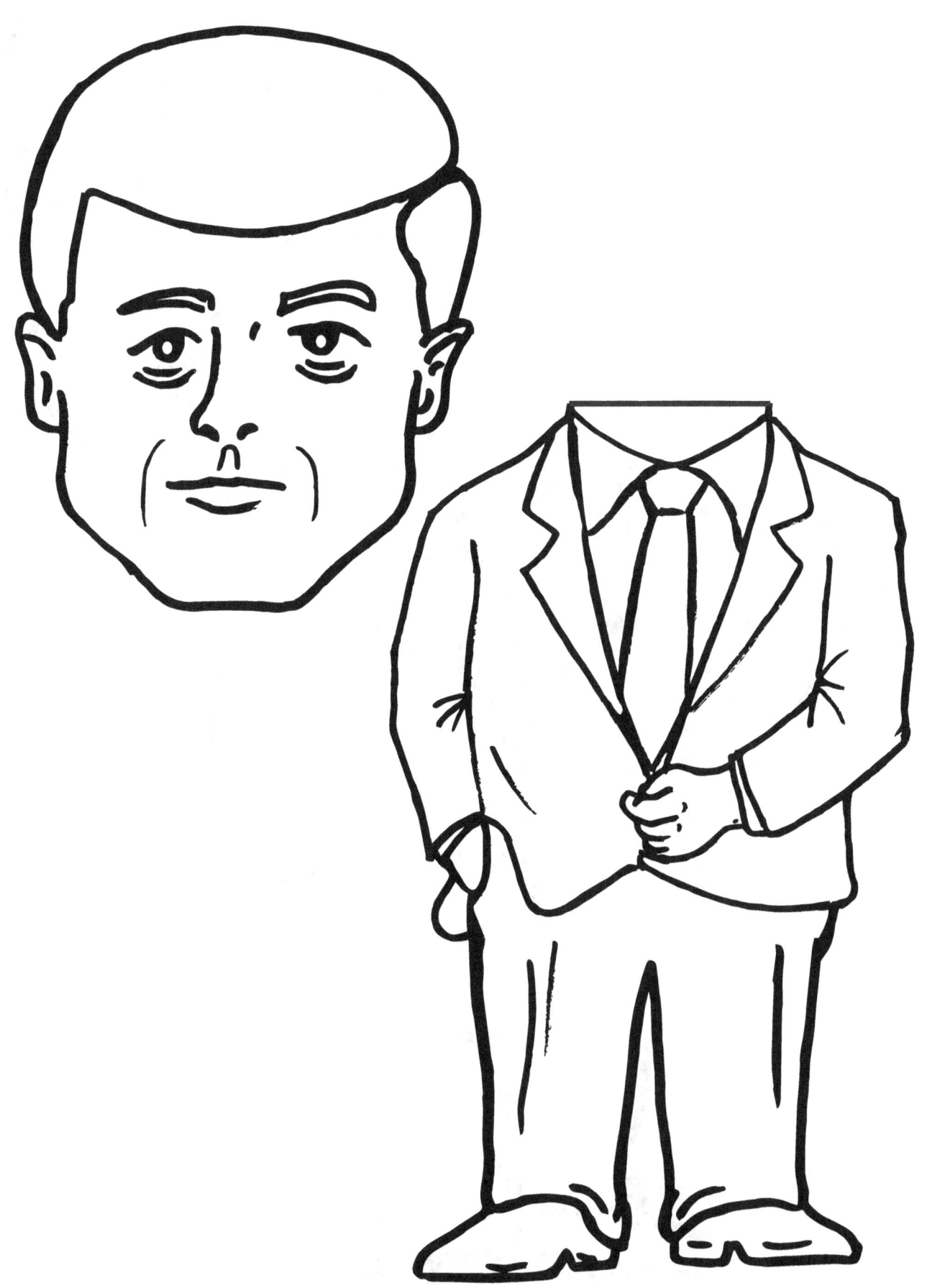

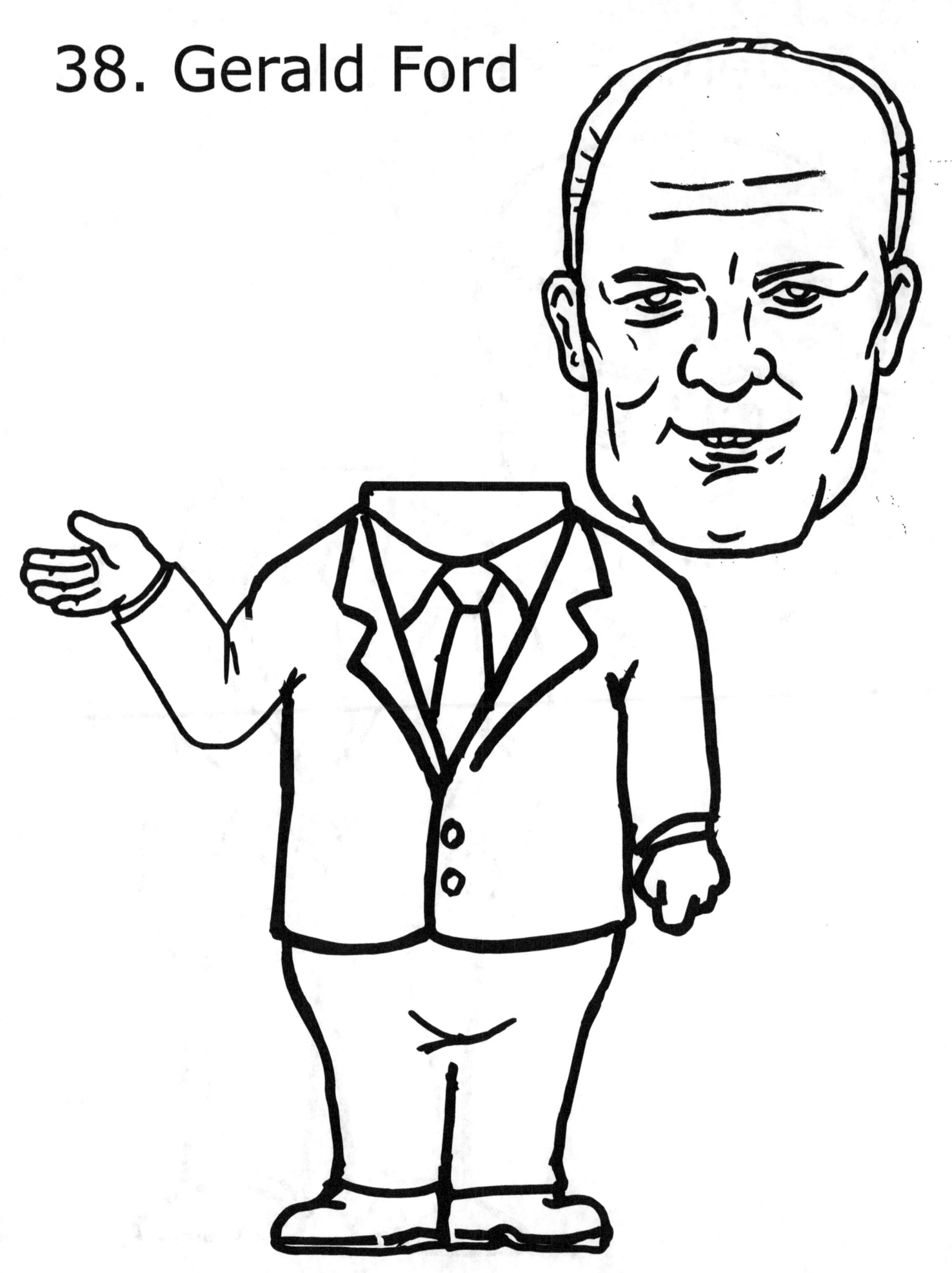

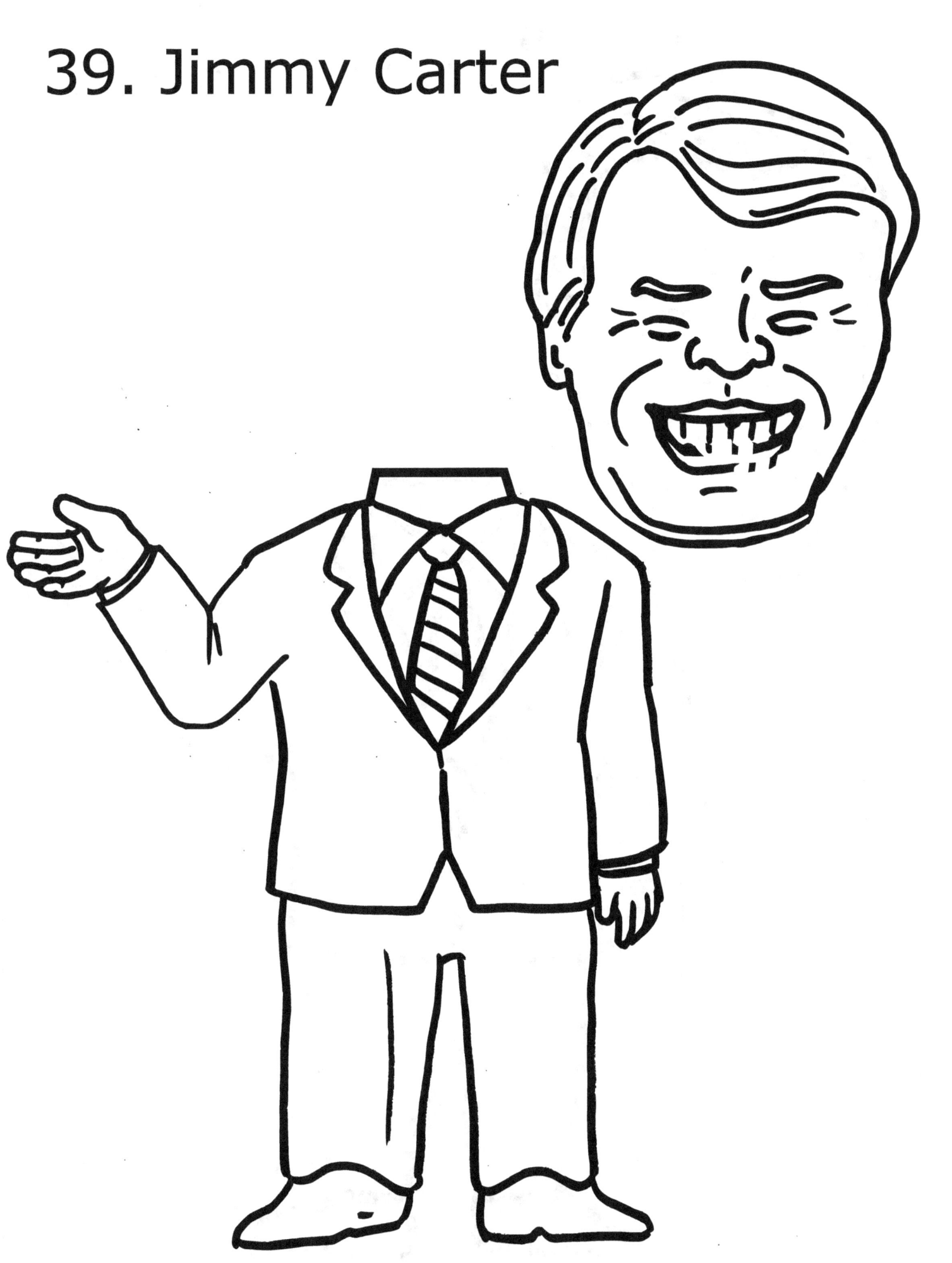

40. Ronald Reagan

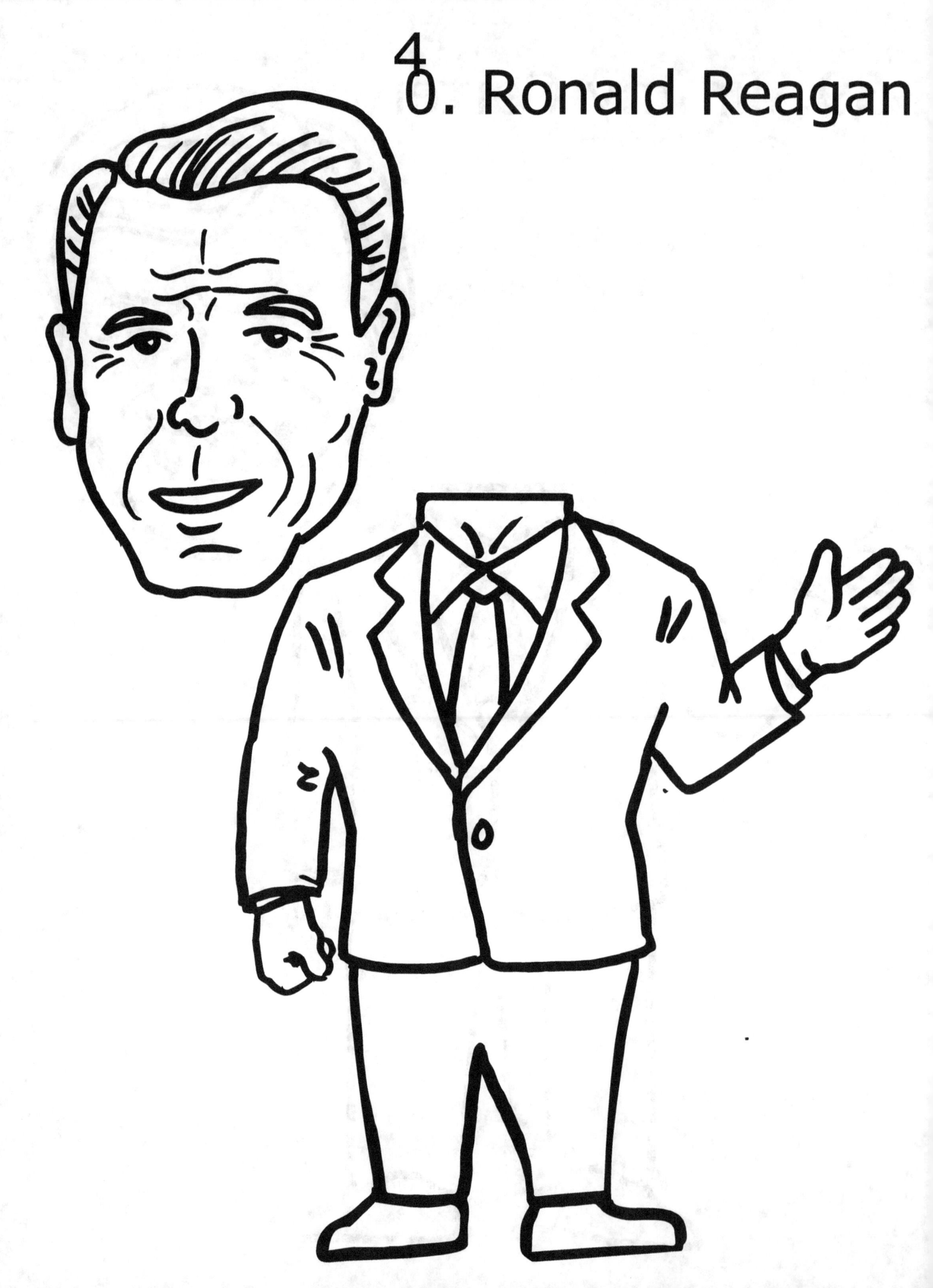

41. George H.W. Bush

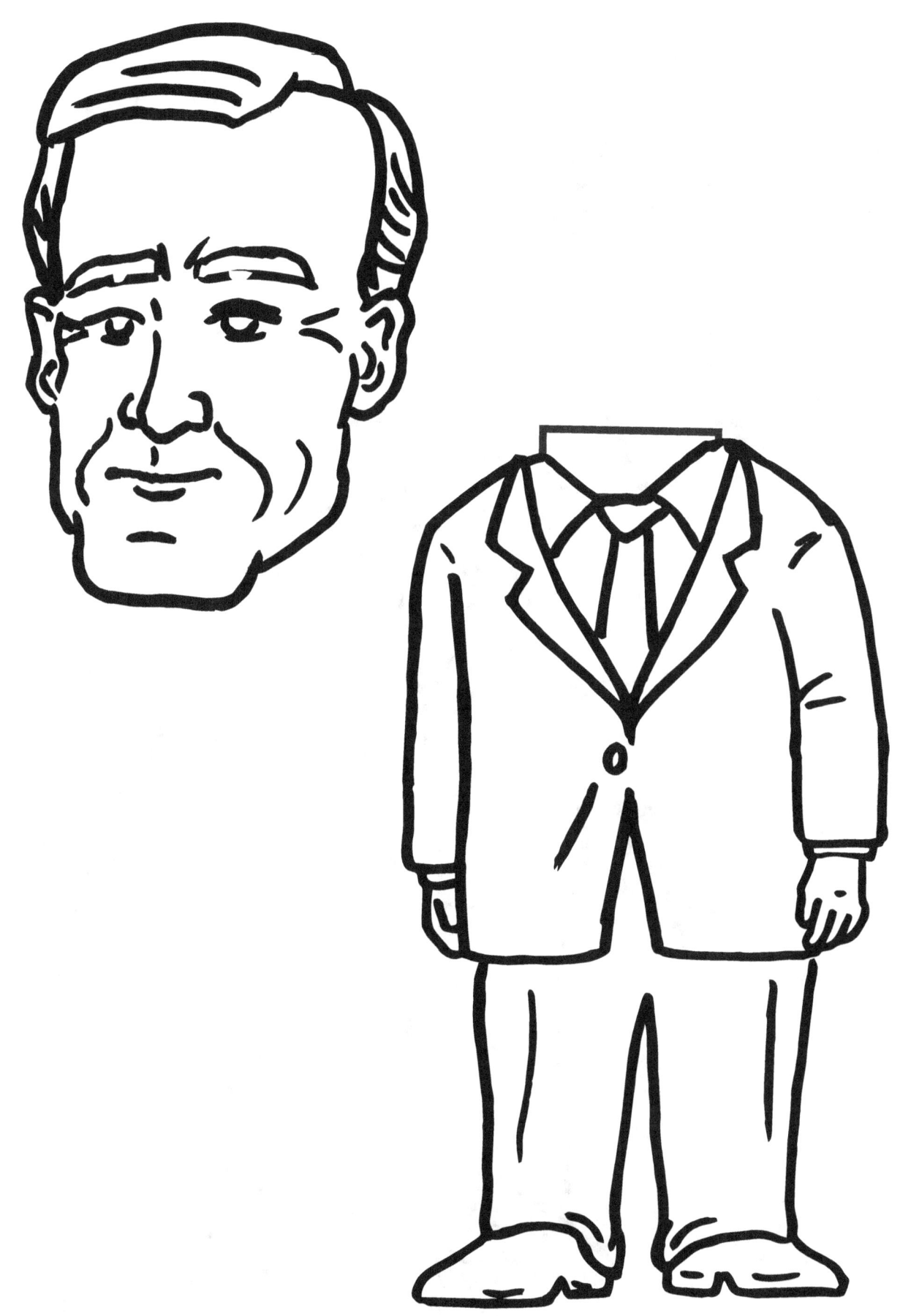

42. Bill Clinton

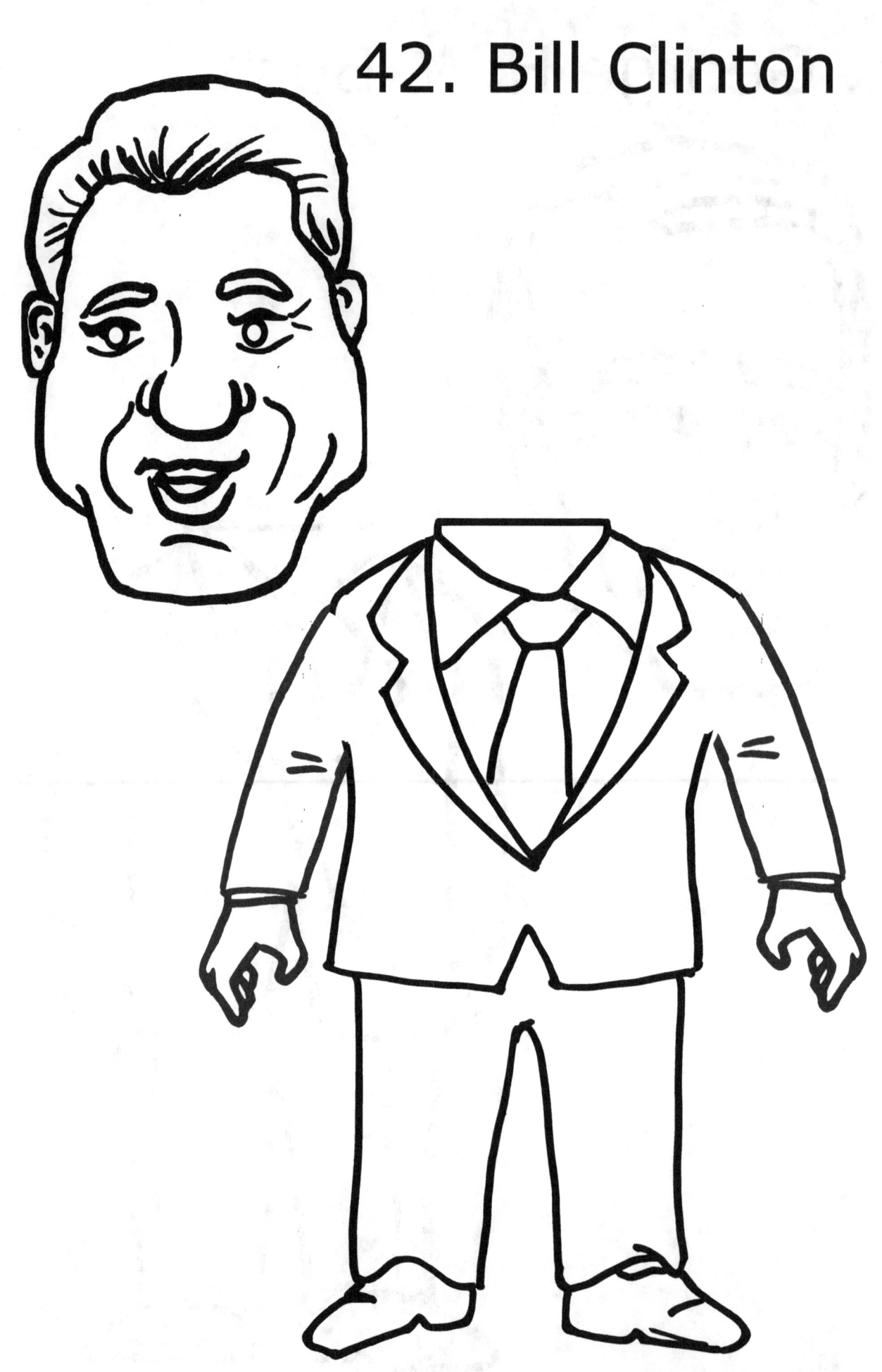

43. George W. Bush

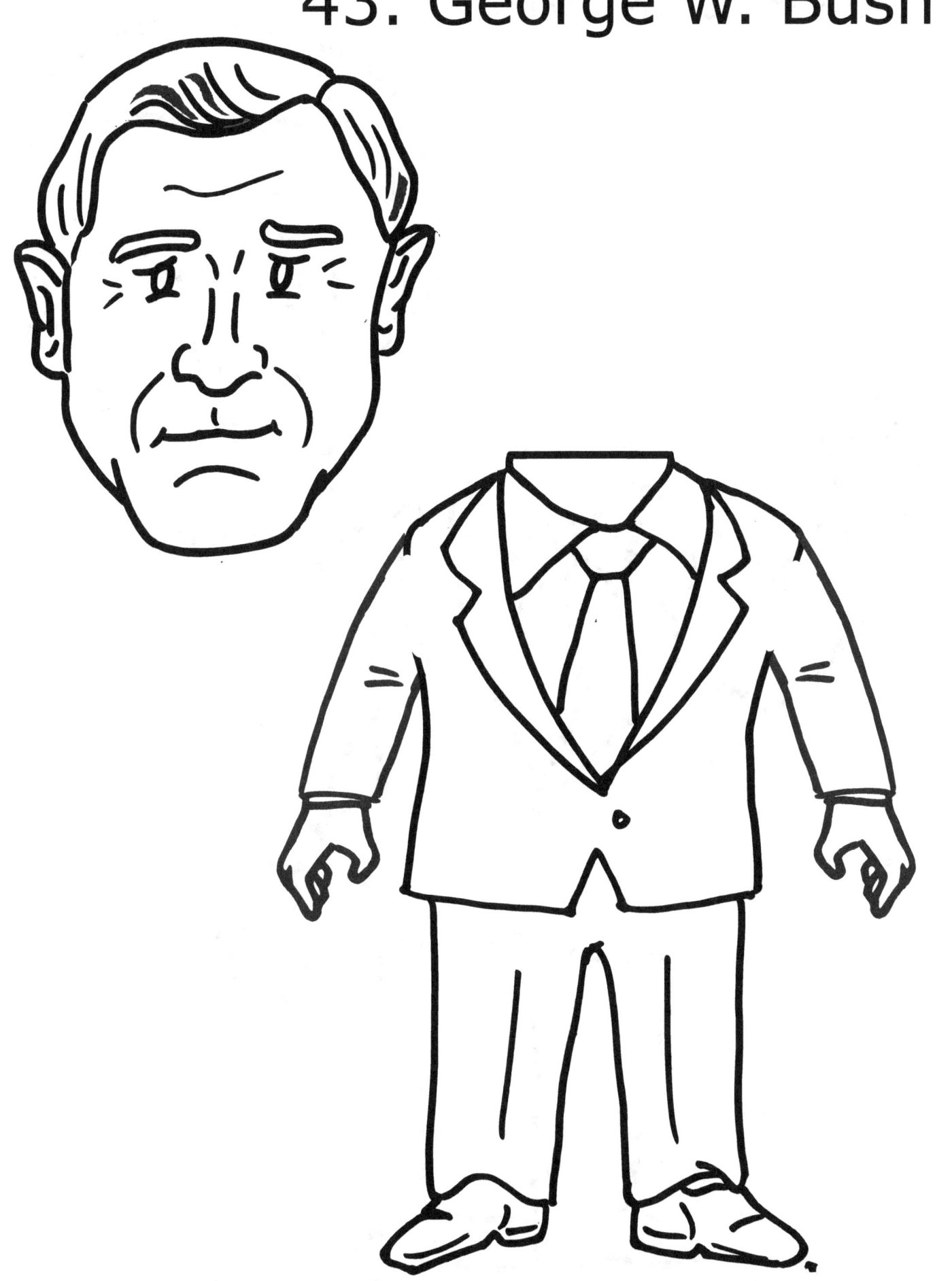

44. Barack Obama

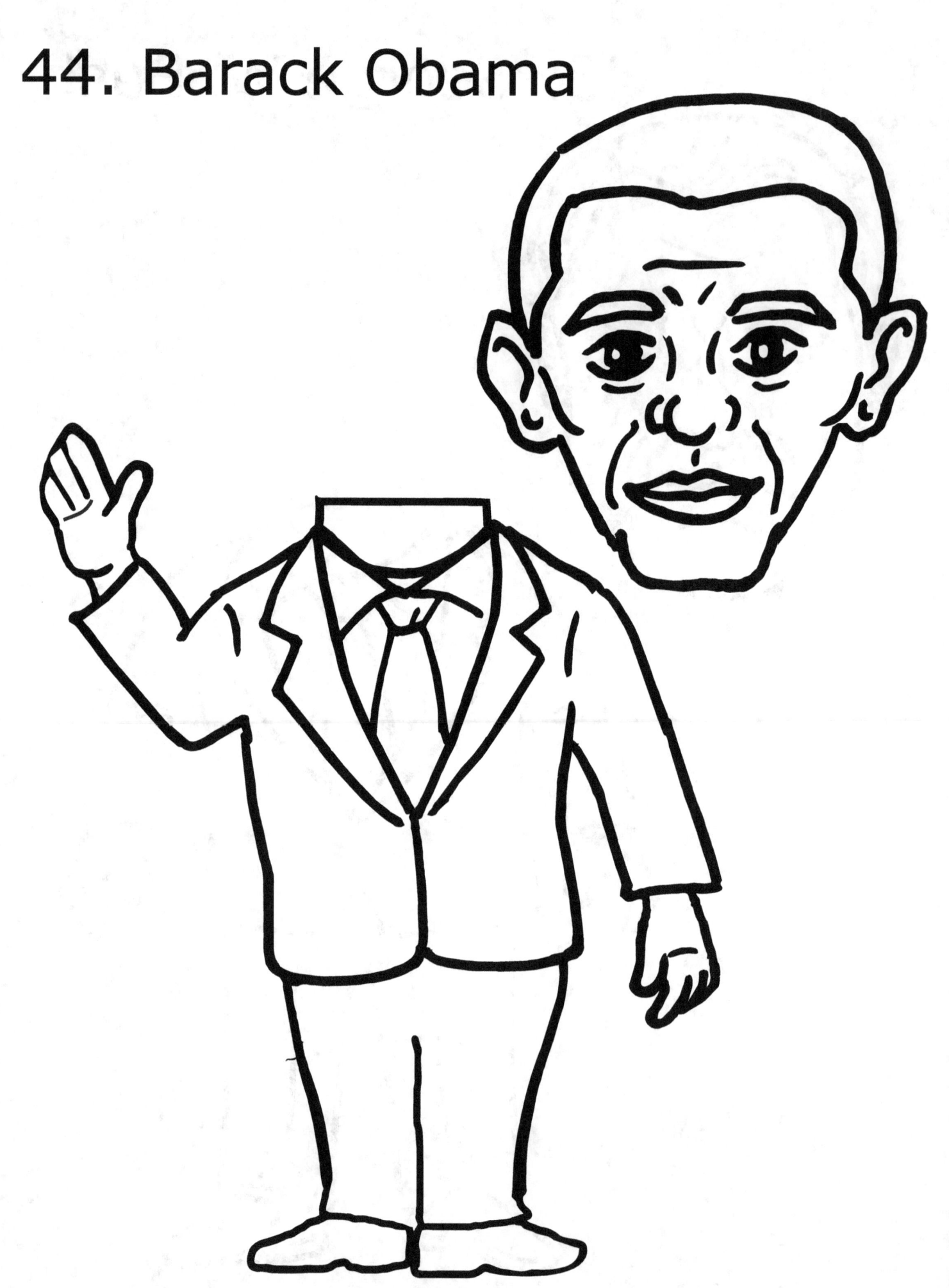

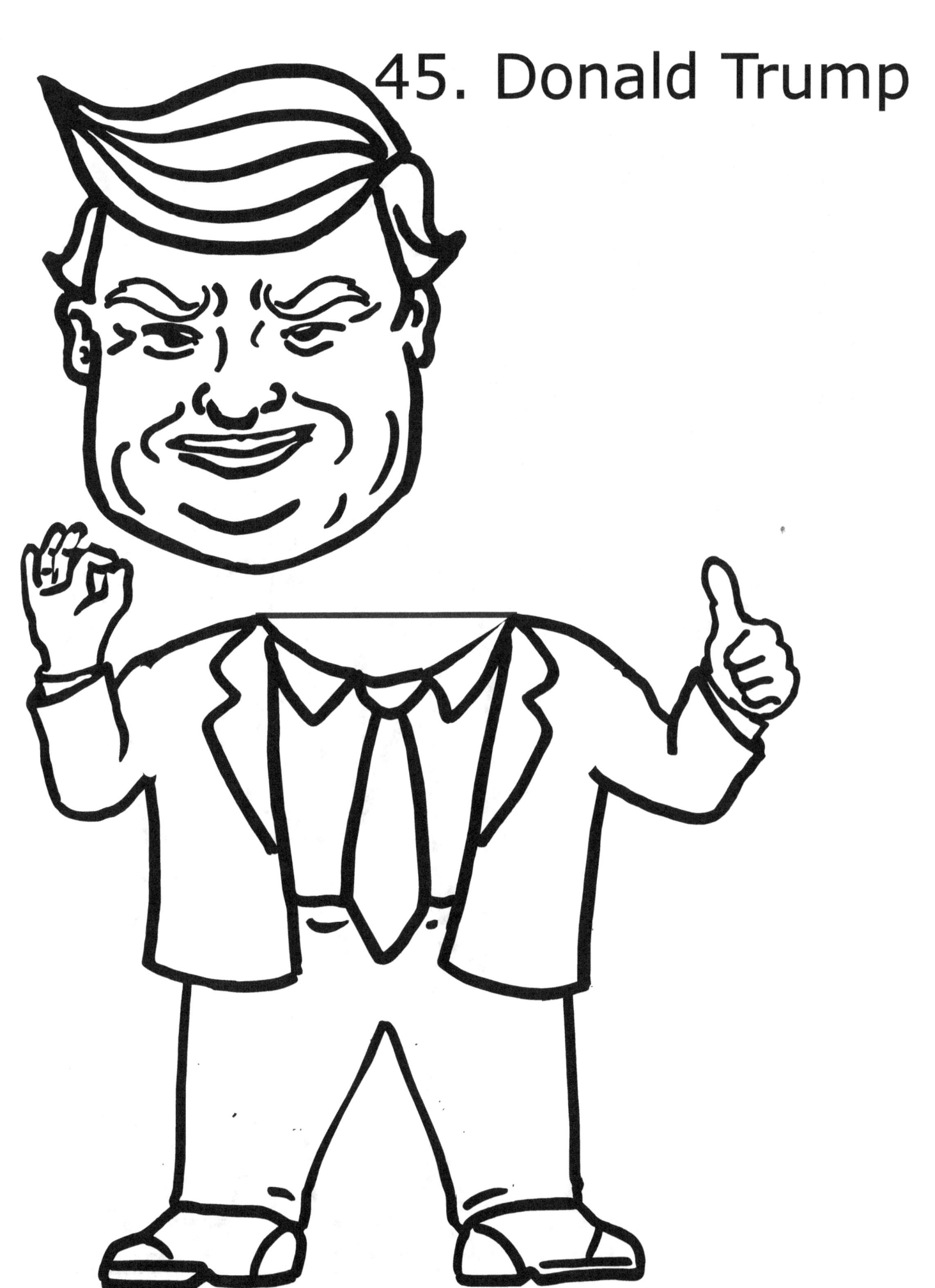

46. Joe Biden

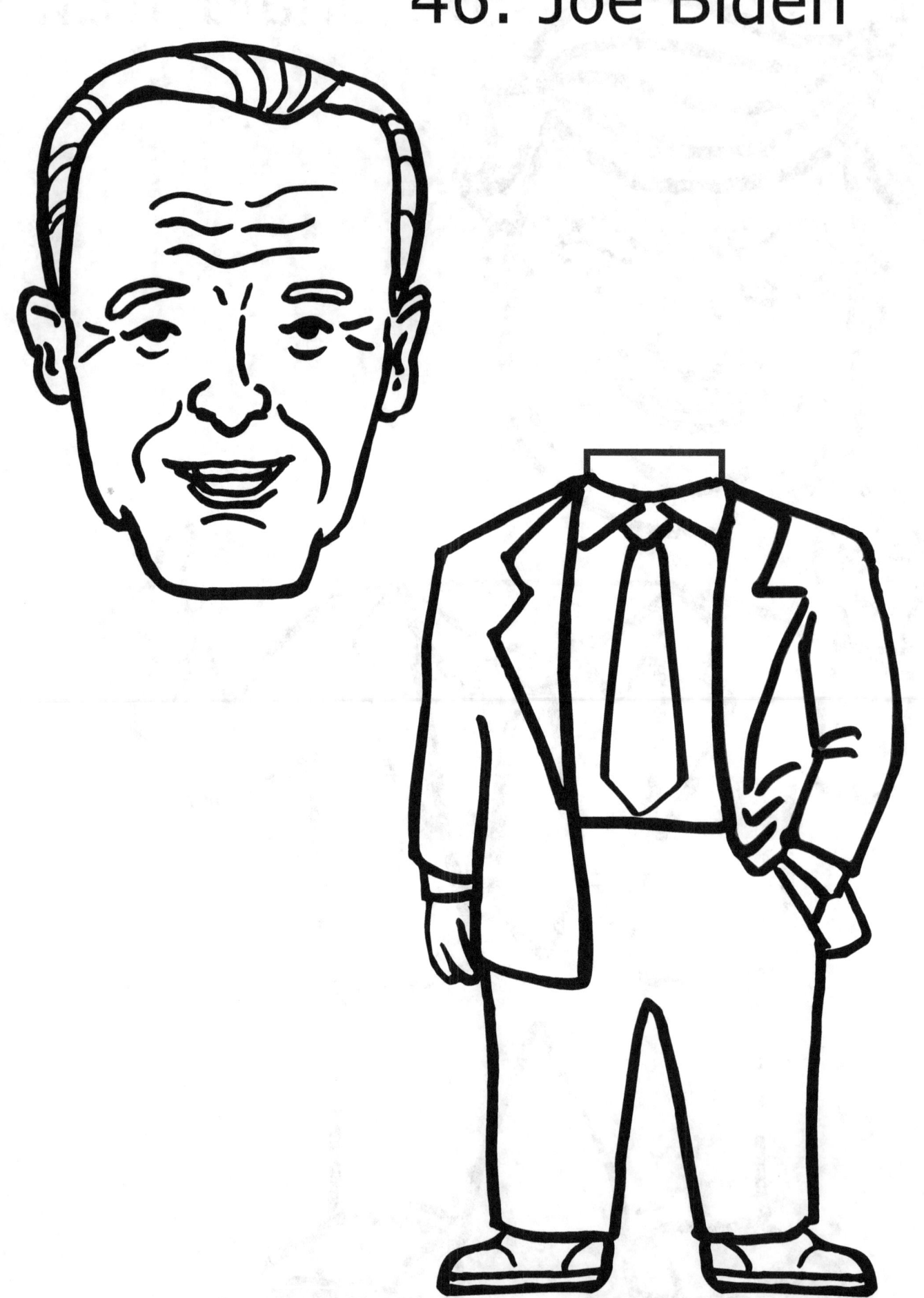

Writing Sheet:

_____ #__

Terms: _____ - _____

Born: _____

Died: _____

Party: _____

Quick Facts

_____
_____
_____
_____
_____
_____
_____

Writing Sheet:

_____ #___

Terms: _____ - _____

Born: _____

Died: _____

Party: _____

Quick Facts

_____

_____

_____

_____

_____

_____

_____

Example:

__Abraham Lincoln__   **#16**

Terms: __1861__ - __1865__

Born: __February 12, 1809__

Died: __April 15, 1865__

Party: __Republican__

Quick Facts

__You may write any__
__facts here.__

_____

_____

_____

_____

_____

_____

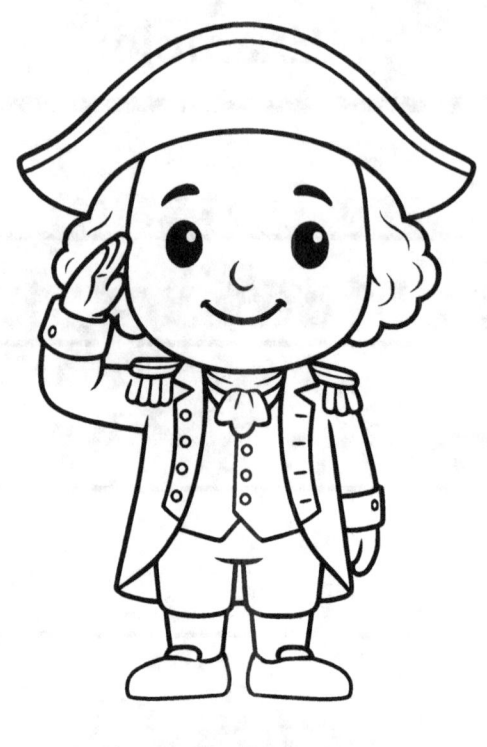

Thank you for purchasing this book! Your feedback helps us create better books. We truly appreciate your review on Amazon.

www.ingramcontent.com/pod-product-compliance
Lightning Source LLC
Chambersburg PA
CBHW080441220526
45465CB00007B/2724